The Minimal Intervention

Lucius Burckhardt

# The Minimal Intervention

edited by Markus Ritter and Martin Schmitz

Birkhäuser
Basel

Lucius Burckhardt

Editors

Markus Ritter
CH-Basel

Martin Schmitz
D-Berlin
martin-schmitz.de
lucius-burckhardt.org

Acquisitions Editor: David Marold, Birkhäuser Verlag, A-Vienna
Content and Production Editor: Katharina Holas, Birkhäuser Verlag, A-Vienna
Translation from the German: Jill Denton, D-Berlin
Proofreading: Andreas Müller, D-Berlin
Layout, cover design, and typography: Ekke Wolf, A-Wien
Typesetting: Sven Schrape, D-Berlin
Image editing: Pixelstorm Litho & Digital Imaging, A-Vienna
Printing: Beltz Grafische Betriebe GmbH, D-Bad Langensalza
Paper: Salzer EOS naturweiß 90 g/m², Magno Gloss 300 g/m²

Originally published in German as *Der kleinstmögliche Eingriff*
*oder die Rückführung der Planung auf das Planbare*
ISBN 978-3-927795-66-2
Copyright © Martin Schmitz Verlag, Berlin 2013

Cover: "Un air rosé" (Pink-tinted Air) was the name Bernard Lassus gave to his experiment with a tulip: he held within a bloom a strip of white paper, to demonstrate that the air glows pink even when nothing is physically altered: a fundamental premise of the minimal intervention.

Library of Congress Control Number: 2022937003

Bibliographic information published by the German National Library
The German National Library lists this publication in the Deutsche Nationalbibliografie;
detailed bibliographic data are available on the Internet at http://dnb.dnb.de.

ISBN 978-3-0356-2530-1
e-ISBN (PDF) 978-3-0356-2531-8

© 2022 Birkhäuser Verlag GmbH, Basel
P.O. Box 44, 4009 Basel, Switzerland
Part of Walter de Gruyter GmbH, Berlin/Boston

9 8 7 6 5 4 3 2 1                    www.birkhauser.com

# Contents

## Editors' Preface

Lucius Burckhardt wrote this book long ago, from 1979 to 1981. The manuscript is a part of the estate of Annemarie and Lucius Burckhardt now held by the University Library Basel. As in his work of 1959, *Die Reise ins Risorgimento,* the author devoted himself in the manuscript to a single theme, in this case the minimal intervention, or in its original Italian iteration, *l'intervento minimo.*

When it came to books such as *achtung: die schweiz* or *Bauen. Ein Prozess,* Lucius Burckhardt gladly cooperated with other authors, among them, Walter Förderer, Max Frisch, and Markus Kutter; but for the most part, he published solo. Writing for a broad range of newspapers, journals, anthologies, art catalogues, and yearbooks enabled him to reach a very diverse audience. A first compilation of this "scattered" work was published only in 1985, when he was sixty, under the title *Die Kinder fressen ihre Revolution.*

Why was *The Minimal Intervention* never published? It is our guess that the concept and preparations for it coincided with those for *Die Kinder...* Besides, Lucius Burckhardt was busy developing a science of his own invention at the time, one that ultimately would encompass all of his research under the umbrella term "promenadology" or "strollology": the science of walking. The idea of the minimal intervention became a chapter in his life's work, and with this present volume we hope to shed some light on it.

A seminar on *l'intervento minimo* was organized in 1981 by Lucius Burckhardt and the French landscape designer and artist Bernard Lassus. It took place September 10–12, in Gibellina Nuova, in the Belice Valley in Sicily, a region razed by an earthquake in 1968. The location perfectly suited the organizers' purposes, for the cities reconstructed throughout the quake-torn valley were the epitome of the planning errors inherent to *maximal* intervention. Alone the highway access road foreseen by planners for Partanna accounted for one-third of the small town's total footprint. In the final chapter of the manuscript bequeathed to us, Lucius Burckhardt sums up the findings of the seminar. We have supplemented this with two later texts he wrote on minimal intervention.

The minimal intervention concept was inspired by artists such as Joseph Beuys, James Lee Byars, Ian Hamilton Finlay, Paul-Armand Gette and, in particular, by discussions with Bernard Lassus, whom Lucius Burckhardt invited to Kassel as a guest professor in 1984. "Un air rosé" (Pink-tinted Air) was the name Lassus gave to his experiment with a tulip: he held within the bloom a strip of white paper, in order to demonstrate that the air glows pink even in the absence of actual physical alteration [see cover photo]. The theory of minimal intervention means: intervene not by violent means in the landscape that palpably exists around us but, rather, use aesthetic or conceptual means to intervene in the landscape in our mind's eye. And the most minimal intervention of all, according to Lucius Burckhardt, is to prevent construction; which, however, is by no means an exhortation to do nothing.

# Introduction

This book is about planners. Planners are a topic that is supposed to be written about in an admiring tone, for planners take responsibility, and gladly so; they are farsighted and prudent, and receive the best education at the country's top schools. Who on earth would presume to criticize them?

Sociology, of all things, is in no position to play the critic. Sociology's job is to deal with socially disadvantaged people; this is its traditional field. Sociology deals with people who are in fixed relationships and make decisions unthinkingly; decision makers, planners, do not fall within sociology's purview. They are not subject to the laws of human existence; rather, they shape them. Planners provide the framework for the life society leads.

The author of this book is a sociologist. He draws on sociology to talk about planners. He regards decision-making processes as a human activity like any other: dependent, ill-considered, dull, and for this very reason, or despite it, describable and foreseeable in part.

The author of this book is in his fifth decade. During his lifetime, the city he lives in has seen five master plans come and go. Each of them aspired to redevelop this city for all eternity, to solve the traffic problem, and to lead the city towards full development, free of conflict. The sole foreseeable factor in all of this was the very factor the planners did not foresee: that such plans fail. Admittedly, such failure was only partly obvious; mostly, it was possible to change the city plan along with the city planner. The author can no longer recall how many directors of urban development he has seen in his lifetime; but since there have been five popes, there may well have been five city planners.

City plans are valid for all eternity; they offer a solution to resolve traffic issues, first and foremost, as well as all other problems. The only drawback is that this solution does not work. Therefore, the plan must be changed, even before full development is accomplished. The observer of such proceedings, a sociologist and hence free of any professional bias, concludes that planners' decision-making practice is mistaken. Planners seek perfection and create patchwork—so why don't they have a patchwork practice? The author suspects he knows why: a master plan is more than just a plan. A master plan has its philosophy, its ethics, its ideology, its psychology, its aesthetics, its politics, and its language. A master plan is something irresistible. Whoever draws up a master plan does truly believe that the solution, this time, will be realized. The thought that it will suffer the same fate as its predecessor is not only defeatist; no, it is entirely ruled out.

The master plan has its philosophy, a Cartesian one, based on the fact that calculations work out and therefore problems can be solved with no loose ends. We call the philosophy of the master plan *ZASPAK*, after the first letters [in German] of the following maxims: define the goal *(Ziel)*, *Analyze* the problem, deduce from this the *synthesis*, draw up the *plan*, proceed to its execution *(Ausführung)*, and monitor *(Kontrolliere)* the success. It is a philosophy which does permit the resolution of simple engineering issues, such as building a bridge or cutting a tunnel. This philosophy does not resolve planning issues.

Planning also has an ethic. As we quickly divine, it deals with responsibility. Planners believe that responsibility can be divided into a political half and a technical half. They declare themselves responsible for the latter half and guarantee that the commission they claim to have been given will be executed correctly. They keep quiet about (or perhaps know nothing of) the fact that it was they themselves who suggested the commission to the decision makers.

Planning also has an ideology: it posits that there are goals and means. The existence of goals—the "solution" to the traffic problem, say—legitimizes the means applied: the demolition of a row of houses for the purpose of widening a road. In view of the lofty goal, namely that all future motorists will be able to drive into the next traffic jam at a slightly higher speed, we are supposed to patiently bear the destruction of our living space.

Planning has its psychology: it is the psychology of the adolescent. At the age of fifteen or sixteen, man begins to gain a complete grasp of the world by devising for himself a simplified model of how it works. He takes this model for reality and tries to eliminate any doubts and contradictory facts. Planners likewise work on models and with a restricted code: they call these plans, calculations, forecasts, and in the course of their work they forget that they are abstractions and not thorny reality.

Planning also has a beauty all of its own: its aesthetics have something seductive inasmuch as they seek perfection. After all, planning strives for the ultimate development, the all-encompassing solution; and who could claim that patchwork is more beautiful than the perfection aspired to? Too bad, that striving for perfection leads in reality to patchwork. Our cities are composed of the ruins of earlier master plans.

Planning also has its politics, its way of making decisions: contrary to the opinion it has of itself, it decides namely, not on the best option, but on the first best option to come along. Planning authorities consist of staffs, and members of these staffs have more regard for one another than for the needs of the wider world. Their decisions maneuver around their colleagues' decisions. The first solution found that does not infringe on a colleague's solution is considered not only the optimal solution, but also the sole feasible one.

Planning, in conclusion, has its own language, and it is a positive language. It deals with pleasant news, avoids anything destructive, spreads no uncertainty among the population, but strives instead to radiate brave confidence and foresight. If a neighborhood is to be demolished, planners call it "urban renewal"; if the street in front of my house is to face twice the traffic in the future, it is called "a relief road." We will be hard put, in this book, to find a euphemistic turn of phrase in any way on a par with the planners' language.

# The Construction Industry

This is not about architecture, not even about construction, but about the construction industry. Construction is a complex, almost a living being, a subsystem of that larger system comprising society and the economy; as such, it has a life of its own. With a tendency to growth, of course, but growth depends on external circumstances. More dangerous still is its autonomous inner life which culminates, owing to incestuous relations, in conditions such as no one with the actual purposes of construction still in mind could ever have seriously intended. Safety, for example, is one field where such counterproductive ills proliferate and can no longer anywhere be undone: fire protection regulations and construction methods interlock in an increasingly illogical way. Plumbing is another field: alleged safety, plumbing companies' investments, and sheer professional protectionism together result in a system of regulations "for the inhabitant's own protection," in which the inhabitant is simply left to foot the bill—or to sidestep the regulations.

The construction industry is comparable to other complexes susceptible to unregulated growth. Even old Eisenhower himself, armament incarnate, warned against the industrial-military complex. Research, armament, and politics—including peace negotiations, disarmament conferences, and mutual surveillance—are increasingly goading each other on in a way that basically no one wants, although there are some direct profiteers, of course. What is wanted or, at the least, partly acclaimed by the public, is the automobile complex: it is directly linked to the construction industry, too, through road building and transportation, which in turn dictate urban planning. The system's concretions are becoming clearly apparent, especially now that the specter of gasoline shortages, long looming on the horizon, is proving real.

Since technical progress in the field of motor vehicle construction has been at a standstill for so long, and the so-called stiff competition between brands of automobile has been limited for ages to merely the trivial features visible at the time of purchase, innovations that would be welcome again today are not only far from being rolled out, but also not even yet on the drawing board. Similarly, and contrary to all the rules of classical economics, growth and capital investment in construction have put an end to innovation in the building sector.

The construction industry encompasses the narrower field of architecture together with its superstructure, the universities, the construction trade journals, the ideologies of the architects' associations, and—not to be overlooked—the counter-ideologies of the young leftists, whose overestimation of the degree of development is downright flattering for the construction industry. The construction industry comprises the entire construction process, including subcontracting by the building trade, material suppliers, and manufacturing industries; and, too, the fields of finance, mortgaging, and real estate, with all their attendant bureaucracy and jurisdiction. Last but not least, it includes large sections of the body politic—the state—which is not only by far its largest client, but also a deeply entangled authority shored up by the legislation and regulatory norms ensuing from its officials' intensive cooperation with the professional associations. The very fact that any progress made is immediately established as the norm endangers further progress inasmuch as it keeps the direction of development fixed, and the currently attainable maximum concurrent with the tolerated minimum. Experimenting with alternatives therefore becomes impossible. Another area of entanglement, already touched on above, is urban planning, where the supposed demands of transportation, in combination with the special modes of financing favorable to cities, lead to incessant urban demolition and, hence, a most welcome full order book for the construction industry—a complex that has shaped like no other the look of the postwar landscape.

In the early postwar years, the effects of this state-and-construction-industry entanglement could still appear unintentional, as a glitch arising from the prevailing conditions. At the latest by 1958, however, it had become clear also in Europe that the United States' lead was due not solely to private initiative but also to the cooperative guiding hand of the state, which, by gearing research to rearmament, diplomacy to sales, and, finally, transportation planning to the general mobility and availability of labor, had reforged the very notion of the state: the erstwhile client now fathered its own projects, so to speak, filling order books itself and driving production.

It was the era of discoveries by Colin Clark and Jean Fourastié. The industrial age was over, or so people thought, and automation was shrinking the job market. Once automated, production above all requires monitoring, management, and distribution: the tertiary sector. This was believed to be a non-rationalized sector, and to the planners of that era it looked like an immense general staff permanently caught up in brainstorming, whose members accordingly were in need of a brisk succession of meetings and information exchange. After reading Jean Fourastié, the Japanese architect Kenzo Tange concluded that an industrial nation of Japan's importance needed a metropolitan "head" in which ten million workplaces could be networked. He consequently devised *A Plan for Tokyo* (1960): a machine spanning the Bay of Tokyo and comprising a transit system that would enable any number of partners in this million-strong general staff to meet at will, instantly, whenever necessary. Many urban development plans of that era—most of which are still unquestioned and still in operation—patently failed to attain technological utopia and are basically nothing but qualitatively poorer variations on Tange's *Plan for Tokyo*.

This development was contingent on mobilizing the population to participate, perforce, in mass transportation and technology. This is probably the crucial factor in the technological revolution of the twentieth century. Until the 1950s, participation in technological progress was to some extent optional. Wealthy people rode in cars; poorer people did without. Even some wealthy people did without cars, taking the train and streetcar or, if necessary, hailing a cab. The city was still organized in such a way that the rich could do without the motor vehicle. The poor had no choice but to do without.

Today, the opposite holds true. Cars are driven not by those who can afford it, but by those who have to earn a living; and anyone who doesn't drive, falls out of the production process. The remainder—children and elderly or disabled people—do not count in the production sector anyhow. Participation in private motorized transport has become mandatory. To refuse to participate is considered subversive. Those of working age who do refuse are seen as either harmless originals or dangerous agents of social change.

This universal mobilization for the purpose of consuming and depreciating cars and street space was initiated by the special "partnership" mechanism established between the state and the private sector. It causes existing facilities to self-destruct and, in consequence, order books such as the economy has never seen outside of wartime to fill themselves, as if by magic. Destroying public transit or, failing that, its viability and reliability, is most important of all. Today, only children, the elderly, and migrant labor can be found on streetcars and buses, that is, those segments of the population with no or below-average income. The advantages and safety of the bicycle have likewise been systematically destroyed, depriving young people of their independence and radius of action and pushing them into yearning for a car—which is to say, into complying with the social dictate. The destructive consequences—or are they perhaps causes—in our inner cities need not be detailed here. This whole development is facilitated by a thoroughly novel coalition between the state and the economy. While, until after World War II, the economic liberalism of Adam Smith called for the minimal state, in the late 1950s it became clear to the European captains of industry that the American economy had long been thriving on those much-scorned state interventions. The Americans had been quick to do their sums: increased taxation does not harm the economy but boosts it, rather, since government revenues are reinvested, so the economy wins out in three respects. It is a subcontractor of the state and a user of the infrastructure that its own employment creates; ultimately and first and foremost, however, it is the winner insofar as this conduct of the state amounts to the imposition of a national duty on the entire population, namely its mandatory participation in all so-called technological progress, which is to say, in buying and depreciating goods, first and foremost, cars.

While taxes become revenue for manufacturers, the economy demands that infrastructure be built. We will see elsewhere the mechanisms by which most state interventions culminate in construction: educational reform of the late 1960s ended in an unbridled rush to build schools, the "healthcare industry," a term that must be taken with a pinch of salt, produced a whole string of scandals regarding hospital construction, and, finally, in many a town or city the construction of a theater spelled disaster for the dramatic arts.

The environment, the landscape, and thus also the urban landscape, are expressions not only of modes of production, but also of the ways in which the decision-making superstructure functions. This generalized assertion is still banal. What our landscape and cityscape express, and in which way "the system" shapes this, must therefore be acknowledged. Many criticize the growing ugliness of our environment, but views diverge on the nature of the ugliness. Some are frightened by the chaos, others, by the extent of uniformity and planning. In fact, both factors are characteristic of our decision-making process: society plans on a grand scale, but in many areas—fortunately, perhaps—it does not have the staying power to carry out the plan. Whatever is left unfinished, those many preliminary stages not followed by a second and third stage, leaves behind an impression of chaos.

The construction industry is doubtless very satisfied with this state of affairs. Its aim is not to complete commissions, but to acquire more of them. Yet without a pretense of completion, no commissions come about. The spiel of overhauling purposeful planning before even the half of it has been carried out must therefore continue.

But there is still the free market, isn't there? Surely it is able to estimate what it can handle and to complete it. It does indeed exist, and the fate of Göhner, a company operating in the north of Zurich, is one of its telling examples, or so it always seems to us. As a young man, Ernst Göhner inherited a carpentry workshop and mechanized it in such a way that he was the first in Switzerland to produce windows to a fixed norm. This was particularly profitable, if the fixed norm was invariably called for. So Göhner became interested in producing prefab concrete components, and by the 1960s, he was collaborating with the Swiss construction company IGECO (Industrie Générale pour la Construction SA), which had developed a proprietary prefab system. These components were particularly cost-effective, if manufactured continuously and in precisely the number specified by the production site: one ceiling element, and so and so many balconies, and so forth, for so and so many wall elements. Such continuity was best guaranteed by becoming a builder: Göhner therefore began to build. But to build on a large scale requires land reserves with approved building proposals, which is why Göhner got into the real estate business. It turned out, however, that Göhner buildings on building land that could be bought in the designated building zones of our cities or suburbs did not come any cheaper than other residential buildings, since the cost reduction assured by prefabrication, if feasible at all, was quickly eaten up by the price of land and the time lapse required for the lengthy approval procedures. For this reason, Göhner's company set about buying up non-building land early on, that is, the so-called remaining municipal area. Only where it was possible to buy up and then develop land not previously earmarked for development did the Göhner planning stand a chance.

Some self-appointed realist once had the curious idea of asking Ernst Göhner to join the advisory board of the Institute for Local, Regional, and National Planning at the Swiss Federal Institute of Technology (ETH Zurich). Göhner, by then an old man, did turn up there from time to time, but, unless we are mistaken, he only once allowed himself to get carried away and speak his mind. It went something like this: "Planning, what does planning even mean? Local planning, regional planning, and so on? I flee planning, for it's what drives me and my residential developments so far away from the tenants' places of work. And while people criticize the fact that my tenants have to commute such long distances, the real reason is that cities' ambit is pre-planned. If you want to do anything big in Switzerland, you can't get involved with planning." Spoke thus, and then continued to chew on the match he had stuck between his teeth at the start of the meeting.

So, Göhner's housing estates are also preliminary stages of a sort, the debris of a great urban utopia that never materialized. Ideologically, this big-city dream was about living in the countryside while working on the metropolitan general staff. In practice, this big city was born of the booming large-scale enterprises' and investment capital's aspiration to no longer settle for the building lots already owned by the lower-middle-class and middle-class circles in the outer districts and on the outskirts of the city, which was only to be had in drips and drabs and in line with the random monetary needs of the random owners, but to skip this stage entirely and immediately buy land on a large scale from farmers. The state supported this trend by constructing the relevant road networks—this was its contribution to making such housing "more affordable"—and the new highways put the cheap building land within easy reach of the city centers. This was, after all, in—almost—everyone's interest: the money could actually be invested in constructing either housing or roads and did not disappear into the pockets of those minor, also-ran capitalists who owned the building lots in the cities. So, industry was happy to pay taxes—for roads and, gladly, for wage raises—in exchange for rents and car sales, just as long as this additional investment flowed straight back into its pocket, without trickling down to the middle classes.

The term "construction industry" is, hence, an attempt to explain these processes of interaction which shape and also mar our environment. The construction industry should be imagined as a living entity, just as [Thomas Mann's] young Buddenbrook imagined the staff of a school [*Lehrkörper*, in German, literally, a "teaching body"] to be a single physical entity; if events are thereby presented as being in line with regulations, it is not to say that anyone concerned is aware of them—but they are welcome.

## Shortsighted and Farsighted People

"Before this decade is out, [we should commit to] landing a man on the moon and returning him safely to the earth," announced President John F. Kennedy in 1961. And when the famous rocket was launched at the end of the decade, Wernher von Braun made himself heard. Asked what significance he attached to this visit to the moon, he replied—doubtless not unprepared for the question—that man's step into space was as important as the step taken from water to land by amphibians, millions of years ago. As it gradually dawns on us, how absurd the costly objective of a trip to the moon was, and how huge are the problems that actually should have been overcome in the 1960s, it becomes clear also that the pose of farsightedness assumed at that time is just as pathological as the shortsightedness of the earlier years. Shortsighted people and farsighted people alike should visit an optician.

After the war, in the era of reconstruction, shortsighted people had the upper hand at first—albeit ones who thought themselves farsighted. Their method was the direct intervention. If the growing number of motorized vehicles caused a traffic jam somewhere in the city center, their answer was to widen the spot. Such measures naturally aggravated the problem, since for every traffic jam that was remedied, at least two more occurred, namely, at the beginning and at the end of the improved section.

Reconstruction—the term stands for an era, not only for destroyed cities—was premised on an image of the harmonious city with the so-called "resolved traffic problem." The unspoken idea behind this was that the ownership of motor vehicles would, as before the war, level out in the population according to income; thus, the wealthy would drive through the city, while the average earners would have to reach it by public transport, if necessary, except in the very center, where they would go on foot. Another underlying assumption was that the income of the upper classes, i.e., of the motorized visitors, would buoy the inner-city economy. The inner city therefore had to be made accessible to a certain percentage of the population, which is to say, those who could afford a car.

The first phase of reconstruction, that of the direct interventions, was carried out in a still somewhat amateurish fashion, mostly on the basis of plans personally drafted by the municipal building authorities and whichever politicians were presently in charge. In Germany especially, they not infrequently drew on prewar or even wartime plans. Reconstruction plans devised by the Nazi authorities in the immediate aftermath of bombing raids were carried out after the war, partly in the exact same spirit. The new axial roads in the city of Kassel, for example, Steinweg, Schumacherstrasse, and Wolters-Strasse, and the Stern intersection, epitomize the mindset which equated wider roads with urban harmony. Annoying obstacles were removed so that the few motorists might indulge in city-center shopping trips without interruption.

Not until the late 1950s did it transpire that the city's aspiration to freely flowing traffic was a chimera. Car ownership did not develop along class lines at all. On the contrary, mandatory participation in private motorized transport meant that car ownership in particular was no longer a sign of surplus income, but in fact swallowed up a significant percentage of its owners' means. With the advent of the first disparities in what I have called the "harmonious" urban model, the stage was set for the entrance of the first great experts, a type of engineer such as we have not been able to rid ourselves of, to this day. The man of the hour then, around the year 1958, was the engineer Kurt Leibbrand, who quickly comes up with a ready solution, in times of war or peace, and provides the cities, for an appropriate fee, with whichever traffic plan they like.

Experts of the Leibbrand type continue to plague us even today. Their working method is of the engineering variety, i.e., they strive to achieve a goal by a certain measure, just as they were taught. We call their method *ZASPAK*, after the initial letters [in German] of the following procedure: define the goal, analyze the problem, then synthesize, plan, execute, and monitor the solution to it. Let's go through the stages of this method one by one.

Define the goal: the word goal alone must alert us to how many social and philosophical pitfalls lurk in wait for us. The engineering approach—"The goal is to cross the river; the means to do so is the bridge"—is ill suited to the issues of urban planning. Firstly, the social problem: Do we all have the same goal? Distinctions between social classes can be traced precisely to their preferences regarding the state's deployment of power mechanisms and public funds. A clash between the goals of the outlying and central districts is typical of the modern city. The inhabitants on the outskirts want to reach the center in their own car and as quickly as possible; the existence of the inhabitants of the central neighborhoods thus comes under threat.

Gunnar Myrdal has pointed out the ideological character of a distinction between ends and means. There is no better example of this than urban planning. Let's consider traffic reform: the goal is obviously to allow traffic to pass more quickly through a neighborhood. The means to this end is to widen a particular street. "Unfortunately," this requires demolition of the houses on one side of the street. We hope the residents will understand that their perfectly habitable row of houses must be sacrificed to the lofty goal of urban development. But there is something fishy about the support for this goal among the building industry's professional associations: the end here is clearly, for certain professions, to destroy the properties on a street, and the means to do so is a "traffic improvement." Which is the end and which is the means doesn't matter a dot to the occupant of such a house doomed to demolition; either way, he must move out.

So, as we see, whoever defines the goal has the power, power that consists in being able to name instrumental measures as goals in order that they not be seen to be means; and this conveniently keeps the real goals under wraps.

The phase that now follows, analysis, is the real innovation of the late 1950s. Whereas the Great Masters of the prewar and immediate postwar period whipped out their fat pencils immediately after defining a goal, planners now honed their growing reputation for "scientific insight" by presenting collections of data.

The experts had meanwhile been to America and had learned there two new words: prognosis and extrapolation. The extrapolation theory holds that the future can be forecast by plotting a series of numbers from the past in the form of a curve and continuing it linearly or exponentially. This, along the lines of: last year the apple tree bore three apples, this year fifteen; if this continues, the tree will yield hundreds of tons in the year 2000. This relatively mindless kind of prognosis was true of some economic phenomena for a while, namely in the period when postwar reconstruction was still underway. It was only in the early 1970s that it finally began to falter, and two terms then had to be introduced to explain the incorrect prognoses: the so-called Pill effect—plummeting birthrates following the introduction of oral contraception—and the so-called energy crisis.

The prognoses consisted of data collections which were taken to be "analyses" of the problem under consideration. Our concern, here, is whether the so learned-looking data collections actually lead to better solutions. Reality is a complex entity and can be captured in millions of items of data. The question of which data is needed to work out a so-called solution can be answered only when that solution is in sight. This is exactly what distinguishes urban planning issues from engineering ones: in engineering issues, the question is clear, so it is possible to devise the solution. In urban planning issues, devising the exact question and devising the solution boils down to one and the same thing; or, in other words: a question of urban planning is impossible to resolve, not because the solution is too difficult to calculate, but because the question itself can never be framed precisely enough. So, we find ourselves dealing with what the mathematician Horst Rittel calls "wicked problems."

In the late 1950s, experts still contented themselves with expert opinions that presented a conventional selection of statistical data in a graphically, somewhat spruced-up form. Incidentally, such analytical sections can be found still to this day in experts' reports. More serious—or more business-minded—institutes, however, were talking already by the 1960s about creating databanks, on the assumption that such huge stocks of data would reduce the subjectivity of any selection. In reality, this only pushed the problem into another phase: while before, reality was too complex to be analyzed, now the databanks were.

This brings us to the next step in the procedure, synthesis. The matter here was evidently to concentrate analysis in a way such that it would serve as a basis for the draft solution. So, data reduction was of the essence. Let's assume that our expert has conducted surveys and divided up the answers according to his respondents' social class, so that his results are representative of the whole city or region. He now knows eighty to one hundred facts about each of a few hundred thousand people, from their date of birth to which car they own (or not), to their opinion regarding future modes of transportation. In addition, he has statistical data on roads, buildings, and the economy. All in all, several million items of information.

However, our experts do not yet have a plausible method for visibly and logically applying to the design phase the large amount of information they collect. We can therefore confidently claim that "synthesis" still consists of the supposedly rational actions of the experienced expert, to which we will return later.

Planning of the solution therefore begins as it always has, with the Great Master's fat pencil. Some "essentials" are fished out from the vast sea of data. They usually amount to not much more than the client told the expert on the very first day. Our city is characterized by the fact that…, The problem of our inner city lies in the fact that…, Important for us is that now, finally, once…, etc.—and which expert would be so bold as to ignore these heavy-handed hints and consider other problems equally pressing? In the early 1960s, expert opinions used to be published exactly as they were delivered. Those good times are long gone. Today, a response phase unfolds on the building authorities' premises, and the public learns only of those expert opinions that suit the client's concept.

The "solution" to urban planning problems generally consists of a bundle of measures, such as the creation of an outer bypass, an inner-city ring (a so-called relief road), and some radial roads—these are the usual recipes. The execution of the plan is now, of course, no longer the responsibility of the expert, but of the building authorities. Therefore, an important component that could perhaps have brought the matter to a positive conclusion is lost. For economic reasons, all that was planned cannot be realized at the same time; it therefore must be conceived as phases. The order of said phases is based not on logic, but on political expediency. This has two consequences: one is that those parts of the plan more easily executed are taken up first, perhaps because they seem more urgent. Owing to this, however, we can already foresee that the second stage of the overall implementation will prove more difficult and be disputed.

Moreover, the second consequence is that the measures now undertaken as a matter of urgency have an impact on the overall system and call into question whether the subsequent changes are correct.

To name an example: If there is any sense at all in a bypass and a relief road, then surely only if they are created from the outside in, i.e., if the bypass comes first and then the city ring.

If, however, a city council decides for political expediency to embark first on the city ring project, which seems far more logical and urgent, and to postpone the outer bypass, it will draw so much traffic into the city center and create such traffic chaos as to defeat its object: the city ring will prove useless. Thus, the expert's solution, although in itself still fairly defensible, becomes patently absurd. — Of course, the experts themselves are not entirely innocent in this case, because, as we continue to point out, they have not learned to plan in temporal sequences. Their planning takes the form of a master plan conceived with an end point in mind—the so-called "traffic solution"—which, once realized, will usher in a state of utter harmony and calm.

Thus, we have shown why farsighted planning is only quantitatively different from the shortsighted variety such as it has been supplanting since 1958. Furthermore, it is based on the premise that a city can function harmoniously once it has been rid of all remediable disruptions. The planned bundle of measures is supposed to remedy such disruptions and raise the city to a state of development that will once again swallow up the growing traffic. The conceptual error, here, is that there is no such thing as a harmoniously operable city. Urban conditions are always conflict ridden, and the planner is always an arbiter between various less-than-optimal conditions. The successful solution, if ever it existed, would have only a short life span anyhow; for technical as well as political changes inevitably take place and in turn bring about further conflicts. Both farsighted and shortsighted people plan for an end state which does not as such exist.

So, now we are at the final point in the conventional planning procedure: monitoring. Monitoring comes too late, namely when the solution stands and potential drawbacks can no longer be resolved or reversed. The "feedback" we hear so much about should be sought not at the end but throughout every phase of a procedure. Therefore, if the *ZASPAK* approach to design is worth its salt at all, then only when it is applied continuously: the planning procedure must be imagined as a chain of constantly revolving *ZASPAK* systems.

However, in the normal run of things no monitoring at all is carried out. Or at best, it is carried out in a way that proves nothing. One popular test directly after construction of a so-called relief road is to measure the incidence of traffic in the surrounding streets; any slight decrease in traffic is celebrated: the "channeling traffic" strategy is a success! Were the traffic to be measured two or three years later, it might well be noted that the side streets had long since filled up again. By then, after all, the "channeling system" would have pumped so much more traffic into the city as to put a strain, in turn, on the overall network. However, the city is not normally interested in carrying out such checks, unless, that is, it is already preparing the next major improvement plan.

## Planners among Themselves

What we have described and critiqued so far is the planners' design activity, and we have acted as if defining a goal then proceeding to analysis, synthesis, planning, execution, and monitoring were all in the same pair of hands. This is an unrealistic abstraction. In reality, the design process is a decision-making process involving various entities; therefore, it is what sociologists call an interaction process.

This process can best be imagined as a broad horizontal line, starting on the left with the intent to take up a certain task before considering, as in a game of role-play, various actions and resolutions as individual instances in a design process which, ultimately, once construction begins, gains a particularly intense and interactionist character. Nor does completion of the project in hand, be it construction, urban renewal, or whatever, put an end to our interaction process. Rather, it is further enriched by co-players, namely those who use the building or the project; and in the final instance, by the building or project itself (if we may say this plays a role), which exerts certain influences, and with which the users, managers, owners, and so forth then interact.

The design work, expert opinions, planning, meetings, and decisions that come about in the course of the decision-making process can be described in formal or legal terms; such a description gives the impression that designers design, legislatures legislate, officials officiate, and so on. Such formal descriptions often serve to establish so-called liability, which is to say, it gets those who really are liable off the hook. Civil servants and expert staffs naturally cover their backs by holding parliament or even the general public responsible. Conversely, however, members of parliament use the experts' supposed expertise to cover their own backs, saying that they agreed to a project solely because the experts assured them that it would work.

Even more interesting, probably, is the sociological account of the decision-making processes, in which the distinction between expert advice and factual decision-making blurs. This begins with the separation of roles once hammered into us in the history class, namely the separation of the legislative and executive branches: our executives deal with nothing so assiduously as legislation, and our legislatures intervene nonstop in the executive process. This, however, is of less concern to us here than the sheer impossibility of separating clients from experts. The client in this case would have to be an almost paradoxical figure: on the one hand, completely lacking in expertise, so that he is able to receive the advice of his planners without bias or preconception; and on the other hand, of such superior wisdom that he is able to immediately weigh the submitted drafts against one another and reach a solution. If ever a client were actually to behave in this way, then tossing a coin and deciding on heads or tails would probably make just as much sense as his decision.

If now we wish to describe the course of a decision-making process, we start at the very beginning, which is to say, in a phase when it is not yet clear, how exactly we want to proceed. The planning authorities, cities, regions, and municipalities always take action to address concrete issues. However, the world is actually so full of issues that we must first of all reach agreement on which of them should be recognized as such and then be remedied. Joseph Schumpeter's model still seems to us the most compelling in this regard: in politics, politicians fight for votes by naming issues and promising remedies. The winning party is the one whose description of the issues is most widely approved.

Comparing issues is like comparing apples and pears; likewise, no objective measure can be used to decide which issues public resources should be used to tackle. We can promote the young generation or make life more pleasant for the elderly. We can improve medical care or do more for education. We can put more money into culture or more into sports.

Municipal politics on the whole tends not to raise these kinds of general question. As a result, it fails also to work out answers in the form of rational strategies. Our aim here, therefore, is to show that the first planning errors arise from the fact that the very way we name an issue determines our approach to resolving it; and secondly, that owing to certain processes of interaction, the proposed solution to a problem generally tends to culminate in a new building.

So, no politician says: We need to do more for public health in the East End. He is far likelier to say: There's an urgent need for a neighborhood polyclinic in the East End. No one thinks to mention that it is because of our modern lifestyles that the elderly can no longer live with the young, and that it is precisely this social isolation which gives rise unnecessarily early to the elderly's need for care. Rather, a politician calls for care homes for the elderly and, if he succeeds in making this issue the subject of a victorious election campaign, will make good on his promise by building them.

So, the first phase of the decision-making process is characterized by naming issues and making a political agenda of them. This naming already contains the seed of what is called the "solution," namely the recipe for a remedy. This process is of a linguistic nature: the vivid appeal of the name itself leads the public to imagine a certain, namely visible, kind of remedy, namely a building.

Issues are not generally caused by a single factor and so tackling them with a single, isolated measure is probably not the most suitable approach. It makes much better sense to tackle them strategically, using clusters of measures in appropriate doses. Pedestrian zones alone are not enough to pull the brake on inner-city traffic; it takes a combination of measures, such as raising the price both of gas and of parking, introducing one-way streets, prioritizing cab traffic, improving streetcars, reducing destination clusters by means of decentralization, etc., etc.,…

In practice, issues are tackled by building something or other, because strategies themselves cannot be decided on, or prove impracticable. Firstly, the necessary measures cannot be coordinated and decided on simultaneously, because they have to be carried out by different organs of the state. Secondly, democratic braking mechanisms are efficacious to different degrees; some measures can be publicly opposed, others not. There is a risk, therefore, that a strategy will be implemented only shambolically, with unforeseen consequences. Construction, by contrast, is generally feasible. From the moment a project is approved, public decision-making procedures are suspended; chains of command become simpler; only in the rarest of cases are construction projects halted or discontinued.

To speak now of the emergence of the solution, the so-called solution, we must return to the distinction between the formal and the sociological description of the decision-making process. The usual conception of the decision-making process is the "decisionistic" one: the powers-that-be give the order, the expert works out a solution, and the powers-that-be decide whether to carry out or reject the project. Any objection that the powers-that-be are not sovereign decision-makers (since they can only say yes or no to the solutions proposed by the expert, who accordingly wields the power), is usually swept aside by that helpful construct, options: the expert presents several draft proposals. In this way, the powers-that-be can be seen to decide which of the proposals should be carried out.

A number of objections can be raised concerning this formal account of the decision-making process. The client is not wholly devoid of expertise; alone the fact that he raised loans to pay for the draft proposals enables him to steer the expert in a certain direction. The expert cannot test in full the viability of every solution; he is instructed to research further in this or that direction, but not in a third and fourth one; for this or that reason, it is "impossible" to do so.

The expert, for his part, is not blind to the political alternatives. Even if the client does not propose a particular direction for his research, he has a good idea of which solutions are possible under the prevailing circumstances, and which are not. Here, a remark by the engineer Kurt Leibbrand when presenting one of his "master plans" seems apt. "Basically, the solution that was ultimately found barely differs from the idea that took shape in my mind's eye when first taking a walk through the city with the director of its planning department."

As for the possibility of options, much has been written on the subject already, and I refer readers to the specialized literature. The ideal according to which an expert presents several equally viable solutions with certain advantages and disadvantages then hands them over to the responsible decision-maker can be called into question for several reasons.

The first doubts pertain to classical logic: the relevant decision-maker would need to have the same level of prior knowledge as the expert; in addition, the expert would have to gradually feed him all the material prepared so far. But if this were possible, it would obviate the need for a division of labor between the expert and the authorized decision maker. This problem still seems reasonably simple, if there is only one decision maker. In practice, however, there are often several of them, each with a different knowledge base and viewpoint, thus representing different parties.

Beyond this classical/logical position there are the issues of how the expert reduces the information he feeds to the decision makers. If the decision maker, in his mind's eye, does not process the expert's knowledge in its entirety, which part or parts of it does he select? Probably he finds most notable those arguments which he already has some experience of, or which are linked in some way with his own position or his interested party, or which are easy to comprehend.

The weightier reduction of information, however, takes place in the mind's eye not of the decision maker, but of the expert. What does he say, all in all, and what does he keep quiet about? Here, we must distinguish between the various forms of selection experts deploy with regard to their clients. Selection can be deliberate: certain things are said, others are not. I once was an uninvited guest on a guided tour, during which a city's urban planner, an architect, outlined for the city councilors the results of an architectural competition—one for a university, as it happens. One architect had been so bold as to envision a system of interior extensions and additions, as befitted an advanced state of university planning in the 1960s. "Oh, you know," said the head of urban planning, "once the facades are in place and bordered by flower beds, you can't have the cranes come right back in for additional construction; it would be such a pity." It was as plain as day that the councilors instantly imagined a bed of roses rutted by caterpillar tracks—and the proposal was abandoned.

External experts don't work as individuals either, but as members of staff; and they are integrated into, and dependent on, a city administration's permanent staff. Organizational sociology studies how solutions come about in such intermingled staffs. Even efficient commercial corporations report that their staffs unconsciously put more value on the ambience within the administrative apparatus than on the efficacy of a solution. Colleagues' decisions, mistaken or not, are respected. Prejudice and faits accomplis are fostered to render irreversible any decisions already taken and to block alternative solutions that favor variants unpopular among the fellow staff members; and any that do favor these are not passed on to the next tier of authority.

The most effective limitation of the number of feasible options is, however, that which professionals call "experience." If we take design to be a process of reasoned research which leads time after time to forks in the road—that is, to points at which different solutions are possible, some of which lead to the goal, others to dead ends—then we can define experience as the ability to recognize, early on in the design process, those roads which actually have outcomes. For the student in class, experience of this sort quickly feels like a straitjacket. Barely has he begun sketching out a solution to the task he's been set and the assistant advises him: "Ditch that idea; the old man won't like it."

This is not to deny that admirable, heuristic design processes unfold in the brains of great masters, at the start of which some options are identified as viable while others are dismissed. But who is to say that these "others" would not in fact be viable? Experience appears to be caught between two extremes: genius on the one hand and pedestrian routine on the other. And given that many of our designers lack genius, an experience of routine is arguably closer at hand; and likewise, an unwillingness to keep on learning among those who already have professional experience and can put it to profitable use.

Our deliberations still concern an early stage of the design process, and are only gradually drawing close to the plans for execution and the decisions thereon, and the construction process itself. Here, that second law of Parkinson's appears to apply across the board; it posits that the more a decision has been subject to bias and limited in scope, the more eagerly it is discussed, and the more lavishly research into it is funded. The construction committee rapidly finds the plans for the new district hospital convincing, but when it comes to buying the washing machine for the janitor of this hospital, all the committee members are suddenly experts and the decision has to be postponed.

The question of so-called savings usually arises towards the end of the decision-making process, namely at a stage when savings amount to but a negligible few percent, whatever the state of debate. In the book *Bauen. Ein Prozess,* we have described in more detail the overall trend with such savings: whatever is considered of general use is usually deemed unnecessary and these savings make the building more specialized—and hence, less sustainable in the long term. That the public sector builds too lavishly, building palaces with public money, has come in for heavy criticism. Experts are supposed to assess how savings could be made on public buildings—any layman can see that there is room for savings. However, the main mistakes, which entail more than a few percent, occur at a stage well before construction. "Build nothing at all, and you'll save one hundred percent of the construction costs," once sneered an architect who felt under attack. And indeed, he was right, for the most expensive buildings are those there was no need for in the first place. And we can willingly list a number of them. This is also why we have described in greater detail the start of the decision-making process, which in our view is of particular relevance.

We could bring this chain of interaction around decision-making in construction to its end, here, with the building. Any real architect turns up for the official handing-over of the keys but sends an employee to deal with the formal approval of the building and then gives the matter no more thought. The building, however, comes to life and leads an existence in interaction with its users and owners and the relevant authorities. The users move in, the first construction errors come to light, some foresights prove realistic, others fly in the face of the principles behind the building. And ultimately, time brings change and the building becomes impractical: it can be abandoned, converted, or demolished. This later interaction phase is dealt with elsewhere, in my work on the historic preservation of buildings.

But first, a few words on a discussion sparked by Christian Hunziker in Strasbourg: he wrote and illustrated an enjoyable booklet about serious errors in architecture, *Graves Fautes en Architecture*. Our commentary on the decision-making process should have shown by now that the word "error" does not cover all that leads to unsatisfactory solutions in construction. But if we were to consider this idea for a moment, we would have to distinguish between errors made by individuals and those made by staffs. This would shed light once again on the linguistic determinism at play in decision-making processes.

Errors are made by lone wolves, great masters, and experienced professionals. Such errors arise because the visionary design never jells as a concept; the intelligence of these designers lies in their pencil, not in their brain; and because they are accountable to no one during the design process, they have no need to put their intentions into words.

Their subordinates, however, insofar as they are employed to draft plans, say, are given obscure instructions: "That won't work at all, you can see that; it doesn't add up. Do it properly!" — This is how these barely verbalized expressions of emotion sound. Staff, on the other hand, do talk to one another—and errors are made precisely because visions are prematurely put into words and never recover from that. For design processes are always in flux and cannot be verbalized in full; and too much division of labor can just as easily lead to "errors" as the lack of accountability and responsibility can.

# The End Product of Planning: The Plan

We have pointed out the mechanisms by which all planning results in so-called solutions, namely, major interventions, usually in the form of a building, which possibly mitigate or at least influence to some degree the problem in hand yet also have other, unforeseen effects. It is in the nature of primary and side effects that all such interventions benefit certain individuals or social groups while harming others. Such interventions therefore need legitimation in order to find approval. They acquire this legitimation by citing the master plan of which they are supposedly a part. It may seem unreasonable at the moment that I should lose my apartment in order that a road can be widened, especially as it doesn't need to be, and will in fact be widened only up to the next intersection; but in the light of the urban development master plan, I of course see the sense of my sacrifice. Likewise, we hope that those who fall in wartime are so reasonable as to recognize that the survivors' wellbeing makes their own sacrifice worthwhile.

Legitimation by recourse to a master plan is part of the ideology of means and ends. In the light of this grand scheme, purposeful lower-level intervention is a means to expedite the master plan. I was to lose my home, not so my neighbor could cut thirty seconds off his early morning commute to the store, but rather to facilitate overall traffic flow, because this would supposedly reduce countless traffic jams and thus—supposedly—boost production throughout the entire region. That it actually drives consumerism, not production, goes without saying.

The master plan thus legitimates structural intervention. If we have an eye for it, we remark on walking through our cities that they are dotted with monuments in the form of master plans that were begun but never completed. What we commonly call the "cityscape" is nothing but the result of concepts put on hold. One good point: fire walls are a sign that someone thought a building line would be continued here. How many beautiful, plastered, flaking, and painted fire walls in our cities—painted over, then flaking again, repeatedly—catch the eye of a photographer schooled in tachism!

Master plans are not "completed"—for several reasons. We have written about this in more detail elsewhere. Firstly, the idea of completion and end states is entirely misleading. The effects of any measures already undertaken—and of all other events occurring during the planning period—propel development away from the presumed objective. Moreover, accepting a master plan had served merely as justification from the start. Dogmatism or perhaps the actual power of the steering body won't suffice to see a work through to completion, once those supposedly approved parts of it have gone ahead. After all, planning fashions change, too, and hence also the philosophies underpinning the master plans. This ideological shift does not come out of the blue but rather from the negative effects of any planning already embarked on. Also, the public is not blind, and the authorities have to fight for votes, which is why goals have not only to be scaled down but also to be taken in other directions entirely.

Failed master plans can be found not only in the field of urban planning but also in university planning, which is of course a popular testing ground for urban planning. In Switzerland, erroneous conceptions of university planning can already be seen at the ETH Hönggerberg (Swiss Federal Institute of Technology, Zurich) and the Strickhof (IAS: Institute of Agricultural Sciences, Lindau). The error in the case of the Hönggerberg is that solely structural problems were tackled. A huge stockpile of buildings was created while the old university buildings in the city center, once wonderfully flexible and multipurpose spaces, were nonsensically converted for one specific use only, namely teaching by means of lectures in large auditoriums. Both the students and the money needed to make good use of these spaces are now lacking.

Cutting the ETH Zurich in half was a bad idea from the very start. But to ensure that the lofty master plan would be pushed through nonetheless, the cantonal government created a rolling funding model that precluded any future objections. In this way, it made Zurich's new university campus a prime example of the fact that full realization of a master plan is hindered not by the vagaries of democracy but by the planners' own incompetence.

The new ETH campus was able to be structurally "completed," albeit not in any meaningful way, because the construction venture was pushed through, all in one go, because the famous 555 million Swiss francs had been raised by the federal government. Since the campus project will doubtless grind to a halt after this first phase, it shares the fate of other phasic urban ventures. Two lessons can be learned from this: one is that we can only ever do as much as we are willing to pay for in the present. All commitments to future payments are problematic. And secondly, the legitimation of any measures planned should rest not on an imaginary master plan, but on an actual need for the measures in the here and now. But how can this legitimation be ascertained? — The answer: by decentralizing decision-making both in time and space.

It is no accident that the campaign for decentralization began in the centralized countries of France and Italy, for their experience of the fictitious nature of centralized decision-making far outstrips that of their neighbors. And this is explained in turn by an even deeper underlying historical reason. Decentralization in Germany, Austria, and Switzerland comes in the historical guise of federalism and is therefore a movement from the Right. In France and Italy, where historical federalism perished with national unification, strivings for decentralization remain devoid of romanticism and tribalism and generally come from the Left. This phenomenon is neither new nor a product solely of the New Left of 1968. Even before World War I, the left wings of the center parties in Italy tried to build opposition to total centralization. After World War II, in the face of the evident failings of centralized governance, the communists and, more recently, the socialists have been the ones to try to address the needs of the people on the people's own terms and in the light of local circumstances.

The city of Bologna in the Emilia-Romagna region is a well-known example. It was a source of great momentum in the 1960s, and after 1971 became the urban planners' Mecca. These visitors were mainly concerned with Bologna's dual focus: on the one hand, neighborhood democracy; on the other, the comprehensive preservation of cultural heritage—namely, the protection of historical architectures, to the benefit of and with the help of the local population. But the bigger picture was sometimes overlooked. Democratization and the devolution of power from top to bottom occurred at three levels. At the top level, by investing authority in the region itself, which is now expected to assume functions previously executed by Rome. Next, at the level of the Comprensorio, the urban-rural association which is supposed to bring the city and its effective residential and growth zones back under one roof, under an administration that is likewise invested with new powers. And only at the third level, below that of the city overall, do we see the development of neighborhood structures on a par with the suburbs within the Comprensorio framework.

The overarching idea here in Emilia-Romagna is not first and foremost to democratize Bologna's urban planning, but rather to reduce the disparity between urban and rural communities by decentralizing infrastructure, in particular Bologna's centralized public services, which are now to be relocated to zones of the province where such extensive amenities are still lacking.

In this respect Emilia-Romagna's planning anticipates decisions that would have to be taken in the future, were a socialist regime elected. Yet as a socialist government in a capitalist state, Bologna can do no more than pursue its plan to equip neighborhoods with equal or roughly equivalent infrastructure and thus offset the advantages of certain locations and hence of ground rents.

It is public knowledge that Bologna's local administration did not go so far as to devolve democratic decision-making to the neighborhoods themselves. Bologna's neighborhood councils were appointed by the central city council and the people on them mostly agreed with the administration's decisions—and could in any case do no more than rubber stamp them. The town of Pavia went a step further in truly devolving power to the neighborhood councils. Without a doubt, it is currently the most interesting example of how to democratize urban planning: a town where the tensions arising between the needs of an individual neighborhood and an administration that thinks in terms of overall planning can be clearly studied. One simple but instructive example is that when the town proposed to widen a street, the neighborhood council responded that it needed nothing more than a bike lane. Adherents of orthodox urban planning theory may very well point out that this shows exactly how the sum of various parties' interests never leads to an overarching and coherent project. But any advocate of legitimating local needs will argue that this is an ideal opportunity to see what the people's needs are, really, when they are asked, really—and when their answer is more than rhetorical. In any case, what is remarkable about Pavia is that here, for once, conflicts are deliberately brought to light and debates are not conducted behind closed doors.

The German Federal Republic (BRD) likewise saw—in the late 1960s—the first locally motivated opposition to excessive planning measures. Yet it managed neither to politically integrate this criticism nor to afford those voicing it a seat at the table; and the few attempts to foster the critics' institutional participation were made merely in order to disempower the local citizens' initiatives and put the clamps on them. In the BRD, local citizens' initiatives and student actions succeeded only when their interventions were truly spontaneous and unexpected. A race developed between citizens' initiatives and the administration, similar to that between the hedgehog and the hare. Citizens' initiatives carried the day whenever they used their imagination to prepare swift actions that took their opponents by surprise. Each time, however, the administration learned from its defeat and noted the trick deployed, so there was never any point in pulling the same stunt twice over. Insofar, any acknowledgment of a citizens' initiative simultaneously spelled its end.

Spatial decentralization is only one means of striving to make urban planning decisions more realistic and bring them back in line with actual events. Equally important is the temporal dimension. We are not thinking here of stages or phases in the conventional sense of that habitual division of large-scale measures into successive steps, for that rests on the assumption that our successors will dutifully carry out any planning we prepare today. We have seen that this kind of phasic approach certainly does not lead to "the goal." Rather, we are talking here about stages at which the present planning ceases to be concrete and it is conceded that the more distant future remains unforeseeable; hence, about stages which must necessarily be followed by new decisions.

Anyone familiar with planning must really be astounded to see how seldom it contains time-related information of this sort, and how seldom the planner admits that he cannot predict the course of events. Probably this is due to the fact that the urban planner has learned to deal with space but not to take stock of time. The planner sees time merely as a vacant succession of intervals, in which the coffers fill up, at best, so facilitating new investments or further population explosion. But the planner would much prefer to realize the end state already, that famous "Z 2" year cited by local, regional, and national planning buffs at the ETH Zurich.

Current planning, in this light, appears to be merely a "time-share" model, a leap from the present moment to the planning horizon. There seems to be little sense of the fact that the time being planned is actually our own lifetime—our life unfolds not in the period following the execution of a plan but in the period of its planning. How blind we are to this fact is evident above all in subway planning, which turns entire streets into gaping construction pits for years, apparently because the streets were previously clogged with traffic. By the time the pit is filled in and the subway up and running, all the businesses on the street have long since relocated or gone bust.

Factoring alternatives into planning—keeping our options open—is on everyone's lips, nowadays. But to decide on alternatives, we need information. The more time passes, the better informed we are and the sooner we can truly assess a situation. In consequence, the best planning of all is the plan to postpone decisions.

Planners accept praise for being "bold" when they make hasty decisions. The "bold" planner is the one who decides a great deal on the basis of very little data. However, planners should actually make decisions solely about those questions which cannot possibly be postponed and must therefore be settled straight away. Their approach should accordingly consist in weeding out the issues whose time has not yet come, since these can be dealt with at a later date; instead of the popular network plans on how to allocate funding, we need network plans that tackle the latest due date for decisions. To defer planning is to democratize planning. Each and every decision is of concern to people who were unable to participate in making it, because they were not asked, or were not yet physically able to do so, or perhaps were not yet even born. Delaying a decision means that more of the people it affects can have a say in it.

Engineers and planners often complain about the public's alleged inability to "stick with it," that is, to support major projects wholeheartedly for a lengthy period of time. Originally, everyone wanted a highway, say, but then increasingly rejected the idea, so that it became increasingly difficult to actually carry out the final stages. Nowadays, the mere sight of concrete buildings and asphalt puts people off things they were clamoring for only ten years ago.

The reason the public acts this way is semiotic. The appearance of structures such as buildings and highways says nothing about their purpose directly, but it does connote further information. The legibility of this system of signs is based on an unofficial consensus that is subject to change. Thus, the first intersection-free stretches of highway not only conveyed the information "You can cross here without braking," but also "This is the face of the future."

Since this "future" has shown its other face, it is likely to prompt the reverse response, namely: "Another farm covered with asphalt." This explains why so-called second stages derive no legitimation from the mere existence of the first stage. Rather, society passes judgment at every moment, in the light of the new cost-benefit ratios—and rightfully so. Uncritical acceptance of supposed gifts of progress, which later turn out to be convenient for small sections of society but harmful for the majority, is assured the authorities only on those odd occasions when they manage to pull the wool over our eyes.

Can we append a section on regionalism to a chapter dealing with disengagement and decentralization? To do so compromises the entire argument; the reader suddenly realizes that the aim of the entire argument is mere aesthetics, and conservative, even reactionary aesthetics at that, just as he guessed. Nothing justifies regionalism in architecture anymore. Why should anyone build regionally, and who for, in any case, now that everything is mobile and every second person is an immigrant, and one, moreover, who is already thinking about moving abroad again? How is regionalism supposed to look, now that materials are universally available and regions no longer stick mainly to sandstone or brick? Compared to regionalism, the

International Style—for all its weaknesses—represents a form of progress we'd like to continue to pursue.

The economic miracle of the golden 1960s did quite enough for the business of progress. It managed to destroy the nation's wealth *(Volksvermögen)*, with success at times, and in part with irreparable harm: and here, I am using the term *Volksvermögen* in its dual sense as pinpointed by Rühmkorf, to mean both the assets and the abilities of the nation.

Thus, when regional peculiarities were abandoned, not only did boondocks backwardness disappear, but also those rudiments of emancipation, self-help, and skillful artisanship hitherto locally maintained by tradition, the architectural repertoire, and the limited yet easily accessible toolbox. But perhaps construction techniques are not at the root of regionalism, after all. In most cases, what makes our new neighborhoods so unbearably uniform is the so-called landscaping: for once the landscape designers have steamrollered us into accepting crazy paving flanked by cotoneaster, everything from the North Sea to the Alps looks just the same. Therefore, regionalism begins where the smallest signs of landscape—a former ditch, say, or a small hillock—are taken as a springboard for the further development and consolidation of local peculiarities.

Consolidating local landscape features—that sounds pretty fatal, yet again. For, as the reader of these texts will notice, landscape does not exist beyond our mind's eye but is produced, rather, by our perception and judgment. That is, landscape is constructed from elements that are very close to "essential" and "actual" things; and this can indeed lead to the musty regionalism of dictators and their schoolmasters. Yet in fact even things nonessential and, hence, the minorities have a right to exist.

Regionalism is certainly a German trauma. Architecture "according to tribes" is a legacy of National Socialism, and the "cultural works" affirming the regional landscape are not above suspicion either. Does it have to be that way? — An architect from another formerly fascist country, Álvaro Siza, handles the topic with far less inhibition. He distinguishes between the abstract regionalism of dictatorships, which is brought about by making a supposedly vernacular mash-up out of supposedly native elements, and, conversely, the realistic regionalism that is forged by an architectural practice involving local people. Such practice is not oriented solely to the local past, but consciously lays bare the tensions and conflicts between classes, between regions, and between construction methods.

"Use architecture to make conflicts visible." — Are these more than empty words? In the case of Álvaro Siza, they are indeed. He built a workers' housing estate in a neighborhood that the Salazar regime, shortly before it was overthrown, had begun tearing down to make place for urban renewal. Among the modest new buildings, some vestiges of the semi-demolished houses have been left standing, as a memento of the stalled "top-down" redevelopment: a conflict made visible.

# Building Stock—The Most Important Part of the Nation's Assets

Architects like to refer to themselves in their trade journals as "the trusty agents (or: right-hand men) of the client." Civil engineers ought therefore to be called the trusty agents (or: right-hand men) of the state, which is to say, of the entire people. If this were the case, namely if fiduciary agents were at their clients' side, then an architectural education would comprise nothing but lessons on how to use, preserve, and, if need be, expand the present building stock.

However, architecture schools teach something else entirely. Assignments are set along the lines of: "a youth center on Paradeplatz." A building lot that has already been occupied and is currently in use—a square in downtown Zurich, in this case—is assumed to be vacant; the task of developing it is approached with no regard for socioeconomic conditions. Whether the lot is available, whether any young people live around Paradeplatz, or whether the city's working-class districts are actually in greater need of youth centers is not discussed. The client's trusty agent is trained to be the client's willing helper.

A true agent would advise his client as follows: Is there perhaps a lot somewhere with a building already on it, which, after some minor alterations, would suit your purposes very well?

Or, if the client himself does make available a property: What changes are necessary to optimize either the building itself or the organization of its future use? But even to ask such questions calls for a form of architectural training that does not a priori entail a new building, but is geared instead to solving organizational problems. If architects and engineers were trained to think this way, the new building would be the exception, not the rule.

Such ideas are still regarded in architectural circles as a hindrance to construction. Yet to have prevented an unnecessary building from being built should now rank among the construction industry's great achievements. Today, bureaucrats and taxpayers' organizations are keeping track of "the waste [of public funds] in construction." And numerous cases of thriftless and irrational procedures in the public construction sector can indeed be proved. The greatest waste of public money, however, is building buildings we don't need, buildings that could have been avoided, if organization in combination with existing spaces had been improved.

There are doubtless economic aspects to preventing construction. Since the general public is now sensitized to the issue of saving energy, we should express construction in terms of calories. This would also do away with those accounting and business factors that make it so easy for prospective builders to claim both that demolishing building stock is profitable and maintaining old buildings unaffordable. In terms of energy, demolition is always a loss.

Property owners who primarily consider aesthetics are perhaps a rare breed. Nevertheless, some among them still think that an old building is ugly, while a new one is nicer, or at least neater. Gradually, however, architectural aesthetics are changing. Until now, only new buildings and so-called authentically restored old buildings were considered beautiful. Under the influence of various art movements and art theories, we are growing more receptive to the beauty of the altered building, to the legibility of the passage of time in a building. This is true not only with regard to the natural effects of time, which is to say, weathering and patina. Emancipatory aesthetic information is yielded also by positively addressing structural conditions under new circumstances, that is, by converting a building.

There is a beauty to the evident thrift in people's approach to new situations, be it the way the early Christian community incorporated remnants of a temple into its church or the way a group of young people has made itself at home in parts of an old factory.

Economics may drive our era yet aesthetic issues are considered vital, too. It is neither the obligation to save energy, nor the protection of tenants, nor endeavors to preserve the building trade that prevents demolition today, but rather the frontline struggle of two aesthetically oriented organizations, which a mere fifteen years ago were granted little, if any, importance, namely the preservationist movement that went under the name of *Denkmalpflege,* and the regionalist architectural movement called *Heimatschutz.* Once again, as at the turn of the twentieth century, the architectural avant-garde finds itself in league with the historic preservationists.

In order to be able to fulfill its task, however, the *Denkmalpflege* must vastly expand its conceptual range and thus also the scope of its activity. This expansion concerns both the building stock to be protected and the "architectural styles" perceived as valuable, as well as the type and the strategies of preservation: instead of "saving the building from the users," use itself is taken to be a means of preservation. Given the sheer quantity of building stock now in need of salvation, revoking or limiting the use of it is no longer an option.

Expanding the historic preservation concept first entails deciding exactly which building stock and architectural styles are worthy of attention. That preservation is necessary became common opinion, owing to the rapid pace of change in the 1960s. Changes disappear from view forever, unless at least a part of their context remains unchanged; overly radical changes that can no longer be measured against the original backdrop foster uncertainty and disorientation. This is why buildings and other elements may appear worthy of preservation even when, by the terms of conventional artistic appraisal, they are not.

However, this renders meaningless that most important tool of monument preservation, "the list." Conventional historic preservation works with lists of the buildings deserving of protection, which are drawn up according to certain principles. The criteria are, firstly, the art-historical value of a building and, secondly, a long since questionable matter, its uniqueness. Accordingly, a mill may be demolished, if there is another one just like it in the same village. Impossible, therefore, to continue using this list of protected buildings, which discriminates against the remaining building stock by deeming it unworthy of protection. Rather we should declare, on principle, that building stock is worthy of protection and demolition always subject to approval.

The "semantical shift" I have spoken of elsewhere has contributed to changing our view of whether architecture is "unimportant." Factories, tenement buildings, and late-nineteenth-century bankers' mansions previously were not only lacking in art-historical significance but also loaded with negative signifiers. They reminded us of unworthy living and working conditions, repression, and boorish ostentation. Due to complex social processes, these connotations have been revoked and partly reversed. The students of 1968 who squatted the villas in Frankfurt's West End formerly owned by bankers not only rejoiced in reclaiming for the people these symbols of grandeur, but also were in certain cases no longer conscious of the original arrogation of such a lordly lifestyle; rather, the nineteenth century, in all its forms, seemed to them familiar and homely, a symbolic contrast to the brutality of modern concrete. Germany's historic preservation authorities now protect the buildings of Germany's Wilhelminian era (1871–1914), which are overloaded with stucco ornaments and represent the very antithesis of an artistically valuable monument; it was criticism of such buildings which honed the Modernist style of architecture. Nevertheless, we find today that these buildings on the whole have a more pleasing effect than new buildings in their entirety.

This brings us to a new tool of more recent historic preservation, which both complements "the list" and represents progress of a sort, but comes in for criticism nonetheless: the ensemble. For

while the term ensemble does call into question the paltry criterion of uniqueness, it still fails to precisely designate what should
actually be protected, and what the onlooker in an urban or village
context actually finds pleasant, namely, the environment. In historic
preservation practice, preserving an ensemble is taken to mean a
somewhat reduced or "soft" protection of buildings yet one that can
be extended to larger sections of the city, to an entire street, for
example. However, protection extends only to architecture, i.e., to
objects that can be protected through building measures. This protection does not say anything about the use and social significance of
an ensemble. That which the term ensemble actually describes—for
example, the petty bourgeois character of a historic city district, the
specific mix of handicrafts and small shops that makes shopping
a pleasure, or rural practices in village life—cannot be protected
through ensemble preservation.

This mix poses a particular problem for historic preservation. People generally suppose there is nothing more natural than the urban
mix of production premises and retail stores, and that it's the evil
large corporations which hound these out of town. But that is only
half the story. Among other factors, revenue from urban land has
always driven the trend to de-diversification. While the real estate
prices in one zone of the city are such that only banks can afford to
set up there, another area is, or once was, suited to certain stores and
manual trades. Names such as Butchers' Row or Saddler Street attest
that this kind of order has existed since time immemorial. So how
does this mix come about? — The mix is spawned by development,
by succession. It's convenient for us that there's a bookstore next to
the travel agency. But the bookstore is "still" there, the travel agency
"already" there. — So how do we retain the mix? — Only by slowing
down the development process while still keeping options open.
Block it completely, and we end up with uniformity again: nothing
but businesses that can survive this blockade.

In aesthetic terms, too, nowadays, historic preservation must broaden its horizons. Until now, it was a daughter of art history and followed its primary criterion: stylistic purity. As a result, historic preservation's interventions were of a corrective nature: it typically "restored" any later addition of "stylistic errors," which resulted in each generation correcting the alleged follies of the one just preceding it. Unfortunately, this game was played at the expense of the old substance.

Today, we know that style is not to be found in buildings, but in our minds. Style criteria change in the course of the history of art; we destroy buildings, when we immediately adapt them to such changes. Moreover—it took an American architect to teach us this—purity of style is no longer the exclusive ideal for us. Rather, it is precisely deviation from the stylistic ideal—complexity and ambiguity—that generates information and thus the enjoyment of art. Deviation can be motivated by the original building or by the later changes. We are mistaken to assume that every building at its inception has an original condition, and be it nothing but the plan drawn up—yet never built—by the original architect; and that we must return the building to this condition. But it is equally mistaken to destroy the later additions. A building has a history, and this history cannot be backdated to point zero. But still, historic preservation often enough wastes its material resources on producing fictitious or, for that matter, verifiable original conditions, at enormous expense.

Finally, a broader form of historic preservation must ask, in particular, why buildings are being destroyed. Wind and weather and the ravages of time attack buildings, certainly; the truly destructive forces are economic and social in nature. Increases in the value of an urban lot—which are driven by the high quality of urban infrastructure—reduce the value of the building standing on the lot to the point where it becomes a liability. The lot can be sold for a higher price once the building on it has been demolished. Owing to this law of economics, the 1960s wreaked far worse havoc on our cities than the air raids of World War II.

Another cause of buildings being destroyed is *Wohnbauförderung:* for, as the German word spells out, this is state aid for the *construction* of housing, not for housing per se. Given that population growth in Europe has plateaued, providing regular aid for the construction of housing is now leading to, and will continue to drive, a surplus of vacant housing that it would take mass relocation to ever occupy. The people still sitting in the cheap old apartments must be induced to move into the new ones. But this can be done, as a rule, only by destroying the old buildings.

# Rationalizing Construction and Dumbing Down the People

Here, we return once again to the construction industry, that mythical beast, which has on its conscience on the one hand the denaturation of architecture and on the other the destruction of building stock, the most valuable part of the people's assets. From 1950 to 1970 the construction industry expanded tremendously. The capacities created at the time were financed in such an adventurous way that businesses became heavily dependent on acquiring a steady stream of orders. Regular orders could be acquired in two ways only: on the one hand, through public contracts, that is, when the construction industry and the authorities worked hand in glove; and on the other, through large-scale housing construction, which for its part required contractors to work hand in glove with the authorities that issue building permits.

Ernst Göhner is a telling example in Switzerland. This man, who originally owned a sawmill and began manufacturing standardized windows, ended up in particularly dramatic dependency as a result of the inordinately fast expansion of his business: his factories simply ran at a loss, if they failed to continually sell the requisite number of components produced. To fill the inevitable gaps in his order books, Göhner was obliged to become his own customer. But even then, things didn't always run smoothly: designated building land, for which the right permits were available at the right time, was not always to be come by. So, Göhner started buying up land wholesale, although we cannot really speak of it as building land, since Göhner's developments were profitable, as a rule, only when he managed to buy and build on land that had not been designated for development. Göhner was accordingly forced to move into these as yet unplanned areas and to play the planner there himself.

Finally, it was vital also to ensure that residents be found for the built apartments. For after all, who would want to move voluntarily into zones where the advantages neither of the urban nor the rural lifestyle could be enjoyed? In the early 1960s, internal migration in Switzerland replenished the population. The big cities were inhabited and their economies expanded apace; population from Switzerland's shrinking zones plus the euphemistically termed "guest" migrant workers from southern Europe moved into the housing estates springing up in a 30 km radius around Zurich or Basel. By the late 1960s, when there was no denying the imminent stagnation both of the population and—relative to previous years—the economy, it was clear that the requisite residents could no longer be guaranteed by rural flight to the cities, but only by migration from the city to the outskirts.

Around one hundred thousand people live along the radial roads leading into Zurich. If this feeder road network were adapted to the alleged "necessities of traffic," it was claimed, no one would need worry where the next tenants were coming from. Urban planning pressure was therefore intensified, to the same degree that the need for this "necessary" urban planning decreased. Urban planning became a means of making the buildings themselves obsolete. And to guarantee that this cycle continues, the urban planning commissions are also appropriately staffed by professionals: Zurich's urban planning board consists of three architects, three engineers, one construction attorney, and only two more or less independent professionals.

Yet the construction industry's automatic funding system is not depleted by the field of urban planning alone. In the following chapters we will shed light on other mechanisms, which we touch on only briefly here.

The first of these mechanisms is the professionalization of construction activity. Construction is the most natural activity in the world yet even those aspects of it that anyone can master are made into a professional prerogative. To begin with, there is the builders' mysterious code: the plan. Plans are the be-all and end-all in construction and yet despite this exclusivity are by no means a suitable source of information about buildings' future characteristics. Originally, they were doubtless more often used to convey the architect's instructions to the mason and carpenter. Today, however, they serve as a tool of communication among architects in their various capacities, be it as the client's representative, the designer, or the licensing authority, and moreover, as a means of demonstrating to the client that he himself lacks what it takes to be a professional.

Anyone unable to read plans, they say, does not see how this entrance was intended. This is how the customer ended up with an entrance he didn't want and that is, moreover, impractical. But why did this information have to be conveyed by a plan? The grotesquely mistaken planning would have come to light much faster had it been put into words. "We enter the house, have immediately to descend three steps, then go straight ahead for two meters, before hitting a wall. We reach the second door by making a sharp turn on the landing and then taking three steps backwards while opening the door"—Isn't that clear enough? Why, then, the mystery of the plan?

Professionalization likewise serves to protect the builder's work, which anyone could carry out, if only the components were designed to be easily handled. We will return later to that tacit agreement between the suppliers of equipment and the skilled traders who install it—not that doing so demands much skill, these days.

Norms established by the government likewise uphold professional monopolies. Precisely those construction activities that the user could carry out himself are subject to state regulation. State norms have a huge and immediate impact inasmuch as they accelerate the planned obsolescence of buildings. All houses which fail to meet the legal norms—in terms of fire safety, installations, and supposed level of comfort—are deemed obsolete. And since the norms steadily become more stringent, any housing stock completed just prior to revision of the norms becomes instantly obsolete. An old house in the city center is up for refurbishment: many people have felt comfortable in this house and candidates are already queuing up to move in after the work on it is done. But: the angle of the staircase no longer complies with the regulations. A staircase built in line with the regulations would practically fill the whole house. Granted, the house in this—extreme—case is medieval. But similar issues arise in the so-called *Gründerzeit* housing of the late-nineteenth century, which is still the most common refuge for low-income tenants. The people in charge make no bones about it: the construction industry can continue to operate in its current form only if all the building stock that is more than thirty years old is demolished.

A final question in this section: To what extent, if at all, does the deliberate disenfranchisement of the user, the professionalization of construction, benefit the construction industry? Here, I think we need to distinguish between the construction industry and the construction trade. If people, also in the tenant sector, had some understanding of construction as well as the right to make useful interventions, extensions, or repairs to buildings, it would only benefit the construction trade and the subcontracting trade. Solely the construction industry would suffer, for its survival depends above all else on demolition as a means of keeping itself in work. The construction trade and the subcontracting industries are caught up in the present set-up only because they are so strongly attuned to the industrial methods of large-scale construction. There are already signs, however, albeit perhaps not yet aesthetically pleasing ones, of a burgeoning trade that is oriented to inhabitants as customers.

When a sign on a small sawmill, one that looks perhaps just as Ernst Göhner's company did some sixty years ago, announces: "Doors and windows. Open Saturdays from 7 a.m. to 10 p.m.," we can guess that DIY construction and moonlighting are on the cards. This gives us hope, even if, at present, some beautiful old doors unfortunately may go to the dogs.

We need not travel very far beyond our German-speaking climes to see the start of a phenomenon that is really only associated with the "Third World": squatting or illegal settlement. Already in Milan and Turin, thousands of working-class families are settling on other people's land and in self-built houses, which is to say, illegally, although this doesn't mean they fail to pay tax or to register their domicile. It means only that they are settling on land they have not purchased and erecting buildings that have not been approved. If we look a little further south, to Greece, Turkey, the Middle East, Egypt, North Africa, or even south of the equator in Africa and South America, we find the same phenomenon everywhere: masses of people flocking to cities and building houses on other people's land. In Istanbul and its environs, 45 percent of the inhabitants live illegally; 40 percent of the dwellings are not officially registered. In Ankara, the figure is even higher, over 60 percent, and these inexistent neighborhoods have a certain degree of municipal infrastructure: water, compulsory education, roads, tax slips, and police surveillance. The latter also serves to determine whether it would not be possible, after all, to demolish some houses without impinging on the solidarity of the squatter population.

Such squatter quarters are not slums, and the people living there have nothing in common with the unemployed population of old cities and the declining districts in large metropolises. In fact, the metropolitan squatted neighborhoods are producing the next generation of working-class and white-collar workers. Here, through sacrifice and effort, the immigrant rural proletariat is rising to the rank of an industrial workforce.

This process must necessarily unfold in squatted settlements, owing to the discriminatory nature of social housing. Social housing is based on the assumption of a subsistence minimum *(Existenzmini-mum)*. We will show later that this subsistence minimum is defined arbitrarily, which is to say, politically. A package of comfort goods with certain characteristics that can be measured and pinned down is declared to be a country's lowest possible standard of living. Social housing construction now consists in using government subsidies to bring this standard of living within the financial reach of a somewhat larger group than would be able to afford it without this financial top-up. However, no social housing is made "affordable" enough to allow those in the very lowest income strata to enjoy this privileged accommodation.

As a result, social housing opens up a gap between the beneficiaries and the strata that are truly in need. This is because—on account of the very provision of social housing—the drop in the standard of living is no longer proportionate to income; rather, a gap opens up between the lifestyles of those who, thanks to subsidies and their own income, are just about able to enjoy the subsistence minimum and those who fail to clear this hurdle and remain considerably below it. Thus, the subsistence minimum, as defined by social housing schemes, proves to be discriminatory: the truly poor person finds himself facing, not a rise in social standing that is difficult to achieve yet entirely feasible, with some effort, but a hurdle: and either he takes the hurdle in one go or remains floored by it all his life long.

We are not addressing squatting because we believe it can help us achieve anything in the "Third World." Our major interest is to learn from squatters how to use houses. The self-built house enables the squatter to escape his misery and move up into the industrial working class, for the simple reason that he can take on its extension and improvement not as an all-in package, but step by step. Illegal settlement illustrates that the connection between home and family, between occupation and existence, is a single process that unfolds over time. The conventional housing offered to us today knows only two stages: the plan and its completion. It is not our intention to deny the grievous fates and hard-won achievements behind any experience of squatting. Nevertheless, we can take it as an example of how existence, lifestyle, and a house itself may evolve gradually and in a harmonious way. Squatters are urban farmers; and even at the so-called civilized heart of Europe, the tales of some person or other keeping chickens in the bathroom of a social housing project cry out to be heard. Squatting is a means to access the city not only financially, but also culturally. Farmers are becoming city people; and in this case, they can do so at their own pace.

Two more brief remarks on squatting, before deducing how we might usefully apply it to our own circumstances. We don't intend to romanticize squatting; it is not a means to undermine capitalism. Rather, squatting is a phenomenon within capitalism. Even, it is triggered in part by capitalism, although it may equally well occur in socialist countries. In consequence, it should come as no surprise to us that the squatter himself, on occasion, acts in a capitalist manner. Illegal properties can be bought, sold, and leased for profit, and leases can be terminated for profit. We may wonder why the actual owner of the land—the state, usually, but at times also sizeable private landowners—tolerates illegal settlement. Illegal settlement serves in most cases to upgrade a property, and anyone who is familiar with the bare hills overgrown with dwarf shrubs around Istanbul and then comes upon the shady orchards and vegetable gardens of the illegally settled areas doubtless understands the landlord's long-term interest in squatting. And another thing: orthodox socialists proclaim that the class struggle must take place in the workplace and not in the housing sector, where, according to Engels, a normal barter transaction takes place or, at worst, something like secondary exploitation. With regard to the "Third World," such observations are quite worthless. And in our country, too, the housing sector has become a means, if not of exploitation, then at least of disciplinary measures, which, after all, are what make exploitation possible in the first place. Because this way of living also generates costs, expenses—for the rent, the furnishings, cleaning materials, the car that facilitates the long route to work—which require us to sell our labor power in this way.

An apartment is a package of goods, and, if you will, of services and organizations. The basket of goods known as an apartment varies historically and regionally. In some regions, the stove, for example, belongs to the tenant; in others, it is a fixture in the apartment. Move from one region to another, and we may end up with one stove too many, or one too few.

This basket of goods, the apartment, consists of things that are not intrinsically linked to one another. Nevertheless, we must decide to accept or reject the package in its entirety; to accept it, if we want an apartment at all. The goods in this package have quite different life spans: the walls of the building last a very long time and the stove, too, may last for decades; yet the icebox, say, is more short-lived, and the fitted carpet, which we were forced to accept, soon wears out.

In addition, there are services and obligations that might well be short term, but are made long term by artificial means. For example, certain private apartments connected to a district heating system are contractually obliged to use no other heating system until 2020. However, neither the supplier nor the signatory knows how the apartment will be heated in forty years from now.

Making a package of the goods belonging to the apartment is the task of the construction industry, and its purpose is twofold. Firstly, linking long-lasting and short-lived goods serves to quickly make the apartment obsolete. Once the fitted carpet wears out, tenants and landlords can vehemently reproach one another that the entire apartment is by no means newly equipped and probably the best thing of all would be a thorough overhaul, if not demolition.

Tenants, too, go along with this game, because they don't realize that the construction industry always wins out. The second purpose is to invest more and more in fewer and fewer homes. Capital in search of an investment can no longer earn interest by expanding the housing stock. As a result, it must increase the value of housing. It must drop from its portfolio those apartments offering little comfort and invest more heavily in others. This also drives depreciation: apartments which don't yet have a stove with an automatic timer seem obsolete. Wall-to-wall carpets that no longer exactly match the shade of gray laid down last spring by the carpet-dealer architects are no longer acceptable. The tenant complains, and the construction industry triumphs yet again.

The lesson that inhabitants of the highly industrialized world may learn from squatting is this: return to housing that can be gradually fitted out and furnished. Getting rid of the all-inclusive package deal means the apartment's level of comfort can be gradually adapted in line both with the family's budget and its individual choices. Of course, the objection raised immediately is that fitting out an apartment individually is still more expensive than the package deal bought by the subcontractor at more favorable rates than the tenant can ever obtain. This may be true in individual cases; what counts, however, is the personal effort associated with the individual purchase, the possibility of postponement and, finally, the satisfaction of making a personal choice.

We would like to go one step further, however, and speak not only of the apartment's comfortable furnishings but also of fixtures in their entirety. The ones we're familiar with today are likewise the product of a historical development born of the interplay of industrial supplier and the construction industry—not without the participation of the institutions behind the construction industry, namely mortgage brokers, insurance companies, and licensing authorities.

How entrenched this system is, is evident in the fact that it has an aesthetics all of its own. We mean the beneath-plaster type of fittings: pipes laid over plaster are considered a sign of slumming and decline, although technically they are probably the better system and, moreover, could be managed aesthetically, too.

Let's take the two most important of the systematically installed fixtures—water and power supply—around which a well-versed network of clients, suppliers, installers, lenders, and government regulations has sprung up. When we water our garden, we use a very simple, modular system: we combine hose sections and connecting elements, as we see fit. Couldn't we do the same, mutatis mutandis, also inside our homes? — That would be far too risky, we are told. It could lead to a flood one day. — The regulations are in place to ensure that a point of flow is close enough to a drain or overflow to avert risk. Well, now, we had a washing machine installed in the kitchen the other day. The plumber connected the washing machine to the water supply using a simple hose and connecting elements that look pretty much the same as those in our backyard. But the most ingenious thing is the drainpipe; usually, it hangs on a hook above the floor. If we turn on the machine, we hang this drainpipe over the edge of the sink (unless we forget). Twice already, a full washing-machine has flooded our kitchen entirely, but without further consequence of note.

Even total amateurs could tackle plumbing installations. The faucet, its closure, the seal, the drain, the siphon and washers as well as the course of the pipes and their fittings are easy to grasp and could be easily handled. But their potential to be accessible to all has sparked a "pseudo-professionalization." Ordinary wrenches cannot open the taps. The design of the armature obscures its functions and guarantees that handling by laymen does not pay off, since it may end in scratches and abrasions.

The same is true of the power supply, which would arguably be even easier to handle. Almost all components of the power supply are available for purchase in department stores; it is handling them that is prohibited. The official justification is, of course, that a voltage of 220 volts is dangerous and in extreme cases may even end in death. This is true. But do all appliances require such high voltage? Aren't most of them fitted with a transformer that has to lower the voltage before the current is used? Doesn't a car run on 12 volts? And yet a car headlight bedazzles us far more than a room lamp does.

Pseudo-professionalization is our name for the system thus created. It serves to dumb down the layman, the man in the street, to the point where the individual tenant is no longer able to judge whether some damage can or cannot be repaired. Misleading design is a tool for dumbing down the people this way: for instead of providing installations whose logic is evident in their form, design plays a game of hide-and-seek with people; as with baroque fountains, the workings remain hidden, and the surprise lies in the effect. And in order to secure this stupefaction, certain designs are made the legal norm. Social housing regulations demand the worst solution of all, namely beneath-plaster installations. This is why a faulty cable cannot be repaired without first ripping apart a wall. This, too, highlights the goal of pseudo-professionalization: to shorten rental properties' lifespan and rob the tenant of the insights that would enable him to see through the game.

Squatting or building for oneself may well be a special case, an exception, in our climes. But, for us, it is also the beacon of a move towards de-professionalization which can start small in our own households, with regard to the apartment, the garden, and outbuildings. Anyone who deals personally with these things gains and maintains a level of expertise that enables him to see through the planned obsolescence propelled by the construction industry.

# Remodeling: A No-Go for the Construction Industry

The problem of adapting an apartment to a family's changing circumstances over the years can be placed at the housing market's door: anyone whose apartment becomes too small or too big should relocate. This presupposes a so-called normal housing market; the older ones among us can still remember the time of a "normal" housing market, namely in the years from 1930 to 1933. The times of a functional housing market are therefore times of need; times of need not only for landlords, but also, above all, for residents. At any other time, capital investment in the construction industry ensures that a housing market does not even come into existence. The means deployed to maintain this state of affairs need not be discussed here exhaustively.

The normal family cycle can typically be broken down into two phases: a first phase, when the family is growing, is tied up with a lack of money and a need for space; and a second phase, when the family shrinks and—if the family is middle class—simultaneously attains its highest income and has a stagnating or declining need of space. The ensuing problem appears to be alleviated in the case of younger families by the availability in cities of non-refurbished old housing stock; larger apartments can be leased cheaply there, by anyone willing to help carry out some DIY renovation. In stable economic conditions—when wages are sufficient to guarantee a loan—the problem can be solved early on in life by saddling ourselves with debt in order to build a house of our own; the downside being, however, that this leaves us with very little wiggle room from then on.

In the 1930s there was the small housing estate model, which entailed people helping build a very small house type, which then became—per limited leasehold—a property of their own, which they could continue to fit and furnish, as they liked. This allows us to trace how the family cycle described above—in the middle class, the initial rise and subsequent drop in demand for space, along with gradually rising incomes; in the working class, initial rise and then subsequent drop in income—manifests itself in remodeling and extensions. Three phases now become apparent: the phase of overcoming the lack of space, the phase of overcoming the lack of comfort, and, finally, the decorative phase. In certain circumstances, a fourth phase can be observed: the remodeling that reflects a generational shift. All this goes to show that there are three drawbacks to the small house whose appearance is not determined by the occupant himself, namely a lack of space, a lack of comfort, and aesthetic shortcomings.

Lack of space proves to be the most urgent; it is the first thing to be tackled—by adding a veranda, remodeling the attic, and building a tool shed or garage. The lack of comfort, although likewise clear from the first moment on, is initially put on the back burner and only tackled in the second phase, as income increases. In the third phase follow changes that are aesthetic in nature, although not without other benefits, too: a new entrance with a canopy roof or porch; or a more accomplished design for the remodeled attic.

The example shows that the problem of adapting to circumstances can be resolved once we stop imagining that an apartment must be accepted or rejected in its entirety, as an all-inclusive package. It must be possible to once again pare the apartment down to its shell and the various components of its fittings. This is the case, not because we believe that DIY construction is an alternative to housing construction in general, but rather because we regard it as one extreme instance in the overarching complex spectrum of tackling existing building stock cautiously, by means of remodeling.

However, maintaining and remodeling building stock by adapting it to the needs of a family is precisely what the laws and customs of leasing hinder. The tenant is actively discouraged from remodeling because, on termination of the lease, he not only loses his investment but also is at risk of having to restore the apartment to its previous and, possibly, worse state, at his own expense. His vested interest in DIY repairs is likewise diminished. In any case, old apartments are usually leased for demolition, which is to say, it is the tenant's task not to maintain the apartment, but to gradually wreck it. It is here that the interests of the speculative landlord and the negligent tenant coincide.

This brings us to the construction industry's fully broken relationship with remodeling. For the simple owner-occupier, such as the farmer, or the worker in a housing estate, use and remodeling are one and the same: the building is constantly being maintained and repaired, and thereby also altered. For today's construction industry, however, building, remodeling, and use are clearly distinct fields. Use begins only once the building is completed. This also means, specifically, that by the time we move into the building and notice its first drawbacks, the loan is used up. So, we are then obliged to stick with it until further notice, its inadequacy notwithstanding. Also in accounting terms, and especially in the case of public buildings, we distinguish between the construction and the operation of a space. During construction, money is squandered; great ideas that later turn out to be superfluous seem possible then. Operation follows—the day-to-day running of a place—with thrift as the bottom line. Now, no credit is given for ideas. The construction industry is interested in construction, not in depreciation.

Over time, however, the drawbacks pile up to such an extent that renovation and remodeling are envisaged. How does this play out? In the case of an apartment building, the tenants are given notice to leave; in the case of a public building, such as a school, use is discontinued for several years; the users disappear, and the architects return with their great ideas. Even the money so lacking during operations is now once again in full flow. Things we had never dreamed of, because we'd had no need of them, prove possible now. Other things we had dreamed of, however, are not realized, because, in the absence of we users, the architects remain ignorant of those dreams. No experience can flow into the project, because whenever construction is underway, those with experience of the building are absent; and by the time they return, construction has ceased.

Doubtless the negative attitude towards remodeling stems from a certain aesthetic that has had its day. It is the aesthetic of the original form, which is rooted in the belief that the first ever design in its unadulterated purity truly represents the building, while any adaptation to functional purposes diminishes its beauty. This aesthetic has long since waned, without architecture noticing: for decades, architects themselves have been seeking out vacation resorts characterized by picturesque remodeling: How many postcards have I received showing the fishermen's houses on Santorini? But practical application ventures to the wrong place: the architects probably try to include an element of chance in their project, so as to build a "remodeled" building from the start, as it were. They forget, however, that the onlooker regards not this element of chance as a source of interesting information, but rather the passage of time as evinced by historical towns and fishing villages.

In Venice, the new orthodox leftist city government presented its programs for urban redevelopment. It is now turning away from churches and monuments—rightly so—and taking more of an interest in people's homes. It thereby seeks out for restoration those houses whose original form has been preserved; and it hopes to demolish and supplant those which have already been remodeled— whereas, surely, the correct procedure would be to do the very opposite, since those houses that have not been remodeled at all are on the one hand dilapidated, but on the other unsuited to modern purposes today. In parallel, the remodeled houses prove to be well cared for. They are equipped with the requisite modern conveniences and well maintained. Moreover, it is doubtless they which contribute the most to the streets' historical character, by making visible the passage of time.

The package deal defining which fixtures, furnishings, and services come with the apartment and which are optional (i.e., the residents' personal choice) is non-negotiable; and its particular form is historically determined. The construction industry is interested at present in extending this package deal. In the pioneering period, the late 1920s, expansion of the "package-deal apartment" seemed progressive.

In an effort to dispense with unnecessary luxuries occasioned by nothing but social pressure, there was a demand for housing needs to be pared down to a universally binding canon of measurable values. The aim was to raise the non-propertied classes to this minimum standard, but also to simultaneously show the propertied classes that bringing materialist expressions of lifestyle into line with actual needs would lend impetus to the social and artistic sphere. As a result, progressive circles began to criticize home furnishings in particular—taking in their crosshairs the parlor, the sideboard, and the master bedroom with its carved double bed and ornamental drapes. Such criticism persists to this day. However, while it was hoped at that time to interest prosperous circles in practical, industrially produced goods that were not loaded with historical connotations, people today are more interested in pre-capitalist production processes, the individual's own creative work, folk culture, and unique items. Then as now, it was about a return to use value, about things that satisfy needs.

Whoever criticizes other people's way of life, whoever assumes to know the more proper way to live, is embarking on that slippery slope of a seemingly definitive concept of need. Whoever critically notes that someone has means but is using them wrongly is obviously more aware of that someone's needs than is the someone himself. And if this someone then assures the critic that the way of life he has chosen fully satisfies his needs, then the critic has yet another bastion from which to continue his attack: the claim, namely, that there are evidently false (or: pseudo) needs and true needs.

Here begins the classic discussion about the market's satisfaction of need. The liberal position maintains that the market is oriented to needs, and that anyone who criticizes either the market's spectrum of goods or whatever on it the people choose to purchase, obviously knows what those people want, even better than they do. So, he makes himself as ridiculous as the dog-lover who feels sorry that his dog has to eat dog cookies and feeds it homemade cookies instead. The counterclaim is that, since the market produces only exchange value, we search in vain for use values. Yet manipulation by advertising is such that the buyer mistakes exchange value for use values: this, it is said, is his false consciousness.

The reformers of the 1920s and, in later years, the neo-Modernists of the postwar period stood by this second position. It is, to quote Alexander Tzonis, the "welfare" position, which knows what is good for others and imposes this at the least on those people at its disposal, hence, on the poor.

It was only after 1968 that the avant-garde circles moved away from this position and thus found themselves in a difficult situation: on the one hand, they wanted to stop presuming to know what another person truly needed; on the other hand, they still hoped to reveal that this other person purchased a certain assortment of goods owing to manipulation of his consciousness. But how can anyone who no longer knows what is the right way to live reproach anyone else for his lifestyle?

The reproach tends to be that the housing of the lower classes today borrows its formal idiom from the higher classes and thus helps maintain the dominance of this ruling class. It is, so to speak, the black frock coat that the peasant wears on feast days: the peasant's desire to follow urban fashion may raise a laugh from the urban dweller, but it expresses a desire for social integration and so simply confirms the peasant's diminished social status.

By analogy, this means that today's apartment is the shrunken form of the differentiated upper-middle-class apartment. It also explains the paradox that today, although more people have more space than ever before, they all still feel cramped by their circumstances. For they measure space not by what they used to have, but by the extent to which they still fall short of their ideal home. And to the extent that they feel cramped, they are diminished in status. Social conditions are formed by the fact that needs are culturally shaped. Our need to satisfy hunger does not lead to us raiding the icebox at home, but to having a meal in the right place at the right time and in the right form. Likewise, the need for housing leads to a social performance: housing means something, we might say; housing is a language. With our apartment we forge a setting in which we see ourselves, and also are seen by others, in social terms. Against the backdrop of our own apartment, we can present ourselves as we would like to be seen in terms of our social standing, and our visitors play along with that.

But while housing has social meaning in this way, that is, while it does impart information, it is also subject to the law of information: it needs a degree of redundancy—which in the case of housing is the imitation of role models.

Beyond the housing package deal, which includes fittings, fixtures, and appliances, the ways in which housing is organized play a role in this communication, in the language of housing. We are talking about cleanliness and order. These are important symbols for the way we live, and are justified at different times by recourse to different arguments. Cleanliness existed long before hygiene, long before the fear that dirt causes bacterial infection. And the way dirt is combated even today is such that the proliferation of bacteria is by no means curbed—just take vacuum cleaning, for example. Often, the sense of dirt is associated with certain other symbols: for example, many people firmly believe that the younger generation's long hair is dirty, although probably no previous generation has ever used quite so much shampoo.

Nevertheless, the courage to be dirty has grown since 1968, if we are not mistaken; and in parallel, admittedly, so has the split between the allegedly clean lifestyle, still caught up in Persil fetishism, and the pioneers who reject Persil. There is probably more political emancipation in turning our backs on the brightly scrubbed stainless steel kitchen than in turning our backs on showpiece furniture. Reason in relation to the excessive consumption of cleaning agents integrates personal emancipation into the broader discourse on leading an environmentally friendly lifestyle, which in turn is a critique of how our needs are manipulated by an industry that speculates on mere advertising.

## What People Supposedly Need

In general, any discussion of an apartment's proper form and fittings, particularly if it is one built by a social housing program, is framed by an idea of human needs. However, this entire discussion is still caught up in the concepts of welfare that prevailed in the 1920s. Whatever the philosophy underpinning each of these concepts, some professionals or other always claim to know all about the needs of some people or other, whom they have actually never set eyes on.

The catchphrase "each to his needs" charitably covers up the fundamental antinomy at the heart of the idea of need. For the phrase can be taken to mean that everyone should be given the same amount or, conversely, that some people have a right to preferential treatment since they are, so to speak, endowed by nature with different needs. In practice, such preferential treatment accrues to those of a social class who know best how to express their supposed needs. No wonder, therefore, that aspirations to certain living standards and lifestyles gradually come to resemble those pursued by the young and progressively upbeat married couples among the new middle-class, who are preparing themselves for a state-funded academic career with lifelong tenure: the classic, middle-class layout, with student-inspired, bourgeois-bohemian touches.

The social housing program of the 1920s and then again, during the critical years, worked with the idea of the subsistence minimum *(Existenzminimum);* and this, in line with the idea that there is a fixed set of measurable needs that must in any case be "satisfied."

This, too, raises a problematic issue that we might well describe as an antinomy. Both sentences are correct: the subsistence minimum is below the subsistence minimum; the subsistence minimum is always above the subsistence minimum.

Every definition of a measurable norm, which is what the subsistence minimum seeks to describe, is arbitrary and, therefore, political. If we look at how the poorest Central Europeans are housed and describe their living conditions as unbearable, we must expect to be told that people in other countries have a far lower standard of living. The average living space allotted to a Hong Kong resident is two square meters. And to anyone who thinks like a racist and believes that Europeans have different needs from Asians, we retort that our ancestors not so very long ago, in the early days of industrialization, lived in far worse conditions than the class living below the permitted standard does today.

The subsistence level of course always references a particular society at a particular moment in history. The conditions it describes are not biologically existential, but social. Man has a right to be able to live in a way that is perceived as adequate in the society in question; but it is highly debatable whether defining a subsistence minimum suffices to assure that he can.

We have already seen in our reflections on squatting that setting a subsistence level—without guaranteeing everyone this basic provision—has a discriminatory effect. A gap opens up between those who just about meet this minimum and thus get to enjoy social housing, and those who continue to live below this standard.

But let's assume there is a country in which "all" residents get to enjoy at least the subsistence minimum. In such a country, a very large segment of the population would be housed under similar living conditions, with some paying the rent themselves and others being subsidized. Above this majority population provided for equally, in terms of housing, there would still be the social pyramid of those able to afford themselves loftier housing needs. — It is possible that England, or at least London, (if we leave aside certain squatting and slum problems), comes relatively close to this ideal model, in some respects. The yawning gap then no longer opens up between the subsistence level and the class below it (the latter in any case having disappeared, or so we imagine), but between the subsistence level and the class above it, a class which can be accessed only by means of considerable effort and a reshuffle of the resources available in the family budget. To obtain a little more housing comfort or dignity, I have to move from the subsidized to the free market and surrender myself to the caprice of private landlords. This means first giving up other goods that had likewise made me "above average" on the social scale.

The paradox of thinking in terms of needs ensues from the fact that one of the human needs is to not be at the bottom of the pile, in the society of which one is a member, but rather, if not at the top, then at least in an average position. This raises the question of the extent to which social standing is expressed, or should be expressed, through housing. We could dream up egalitarian societies, whose goals are so immaterial in character that the housing situation plays no part in shaping them. Likewise possible, and more realistic, is to imagine societies whose internal distinctions find expression in other things than housing. Nomadic societies are one such example. In many non-European societies, the degree of importance attached to housing is not as high as it is in ours. — All the more reason, therefore, to take seriously the fact that housing in our country satisfies not only physical needs, but also, to a large degree, social needs.

In the late 1960s, a word appeared that helped further the debate somewhat: the need for "identification." Criticism of the uniformity of large housing estates led to the notion that a person could feel comfortable only if he identified with his home. The prerequisite for such identification is, however, something special, which is to say, the presence of an unmistakable feature that does not instantly prove to be ubiquitous. In architecture, this led specifically to the demand for architectural "features" that disrupt the uniformity; only in the 1970s did this culminate in the somewhat more realistic approach, namely that such opportunities for identification should be created not by the architect, but by the residents themselves.

A work by the psychologist Goffman was deemed relevant to architects, insofar as it was featured relatively early in *Bauwelt Fundamente,* a classic German book series on the essentials of architecture and urban planning; yet among this professional readership, its message often fell on deaf ears. According to Goffman, we must begin with the question of how people present themselves in the everyday life of their society. Part of this presentation is the "setting," which in the normal run of our society is the home or, if need be, the car, while for medieval kings, for example, it was pomp and ostentation on wheels.

Now, a characteristic of this setting is that it exists to a large degree solely in the imagination of its inhabitant and can be made manifest in reality only in part. Symbolic touches made to the apartment and its furnishings therefore must indicate in legible form the far greater splendor actually intended. For the entire setting, as actually intended, must be clear not only in the mind's eye of the inhabitant, but also in that of his counterpart, the visitor. The former's housing need is satisfied when the visitor is able to read the setting and play his role in it, i.e., to participate in the overall fantasy structure.

Take the dinner invitation, for example. We'd like to present ourselves to our acquaintances in what is actually our intended setting. Since we don't have a sufficiently large dining table, we have to put two tables together. Then the tablecloth is too small—so we cleverly place it such that another one beneath it peeks out at each end, as if that's exactly how it should be. We don't have enough matching chairs, either; but with the help of some cushions from the picnic basket we can disguise the variations. We have neither a paid help nor a cook, and the menu chosen is, therefore, one that can be conjured effortlessly to the table by a single housewife. The party is a success because the guests play along. They serve themselves as unobtrusively as if they were being served; and not one of them springs to his feet to carry a bowl back to the kitchen.

The situation described above may sound bourgeois, stuffy. But don't be deluded into thinking that a party any less bourgeois represents relations as they truly are and requires no imagination. "Oh, it's all very casual at our place," says the director of another setting, in welcome, as she ushers us into the kitchen. There, guests are already standing around seemingly casually at ease, the one stirring a pot of goulash, another beating several eggs in a basin while less talented guests set about finding a corkscrew and admiring the content of the kitchen cabinet, most of which comes from a flea market. — This situation, too, describes a setting that is articulated in certain touches or attitudes yet to a large degree remains merely a concept—but one understood by the guests and fleshed out with love and fantasy.

After these two portrayals of milieu, it is perhaps a little easier to think about so-called housing needs. Of course, the apartment must fulfill certain basic functions, also measurable ones: in our climes, the temperature in the room we spend all our time in should not fall below 19 degrees Celsius. Nevertheless, we tend to endure even those friendly hosts who roast our front side with an open fire, in their vacation home, while leaving our backs icy cold. As a rule, human needs do not merely demand to be satisfied but are culturally charged in a way such that makes social contexts livable. The way we satisfy our needs is a language that informs us as well as others about our standing and our demands on society. But the means to express these demands must be available—and to become visible, they must exceed the universal standard that planners try to pin us down to.

Insofar the subsistence level is always above the subsistence level. But of course, not across the entire spectrum of housing in all its aspects. We know how it is when we are looking for an apartment: we have the choice between an apartment that has a sun terrace but stove heating, and one that has a particularly wide entrance hallway but no balcony. Which should we choose? — In any case, one that can be arranged in such a way as to make something special out of it, something of which our benevolent visitors can say: "You have it so good here. How did you manage to find such an apartment?"

Meeting our housing needs should, it is believed, lead to satisfaction. And so, anyone who builds housing dutifully has surveys conducted on how satisfied the residents of his estates are. And lo and behold, all these surveys show that over 90 percent of tenants—which is to say, practically all "reasonable people"—are satisfied with their apartment. Is there, then, in analogy to "false consciousness," such a thing as false satisfaction?

We have already conducted such surveys ourselves; one in a dilapidated old city neighborhood, for example, with housing conditions the likes of which you would hardly have expected to find in our country: houses with six or eight apartments shared a single toilet that was situated, moreover, at the far end of the yard. Most of the apartments were inhabited by old people, all of whom assured us that they were content with their lot, some even adding that their visitors were apt to say, "Oh, but you do have it nice here"—which just goes to show that, even in such miserable conditions, people tend to go along with reading the setting as it is intended.

Several theories venture to explain this satisfaction. One is, that this old city neighborhood was under threat of large-scale redevelopment and the residents possibly hoped their statements would protect it. Secondly, an old city neighborhood has not only its run-down aspects but also some that hint at its former grandeur: it contains, as we have said, the rudiments of a desirable setting. We also consider a third explanation, namely that these aging respondents had another, greater concern than the state of their apartment: their state of ill-health, which each of them was happy to report on at length.

But ultimately, our respondents' conduct seemed to us to be a case of what Leon Festinger describes as "dissonance reduction." — The disadvantages of our living space are overridden by arguments that frame them as advantages or that bring other advantages to light. In convincing themselves or talking with visitors, residents marshal arguments that bridge the gap between the desired dwelling and the sad reality.

This highlights the existential character of the social aspects of housing. The inhabitant cannot endure the loss of social standing implicit in the state of his apartment. If he does not succeed in eliminating the defect, he finds arguments enough to bypass it. He can do so, however, only if the apartment provides, besides said defects, some grounds for a positive take on it. — Probably, this is what was meant by the word identification.

## Device and Form

Modern architects of the early *Werkbund* and the interwar avant-garde concerned themselves not only with the house and the home, but also with devices—and rightly so. By the end of World War II, that urge to reform everyday life which had driven the redesign of furniture, fixtures, and fittings had largely dissipated. In the 1950s, people limited themselves on the one hand to the liberalist catch-phrase "technology is neutral"—claiming it was up to the individual to make of it what he would—and on the other hand to exploiting the aesthetic legacy of the 1920s by means of a preoccupation with what came then to be called "good form."[1] There's no crime in wanting a world in which all objects and devices evince good form—or so the somewhat superficial idea that good form alone suffices to overrule not only the clash of art and technology, but also any other conflict.

Strangely enough, not even the ideologists at the design school Hochschule für Gestaltung (HfG) in Ulm, Germany, managed to come up with a consistent theory of design for the 1960s. On the one hand they were relatively quick to propound the insights of the English discourse on semiotics, aesthetic depreciation, and popular culture. They recognized that every form contains information, and that this information necessarily becomes outdated, after a while, whereupon new information supplants it. The HfG tried here to adopt the "enlightened vitalism" position, which is to say, to see

---

1   Max Bill's book, *Die Gute Form* (1957), decisively shaped the trend towards functional yet aesthetically pleasing "timeless" design. The Federal Award for Good Form instigated in 1969 by the German Ministry of Economics was succeeded by the present German Design Award.

through these processes yet nonetheless go along with them. The products themselves, however, attest nothing but the persistence of formalistic idealism, the yearning for a society that would become more progressive by living among, and in, good forms. — Both positions, however, fail to consider the object itself: no distinction is made between the socially useful and the harmful device.

Can devices "in and of themselves" be good or bad? — The early avant-garde answered the question with yes, we believe, yet its opinion was obscured by later developments, until Ivan Illich posed the question again with renewed insistence. — The early avant-garde welcomed household technology; and this technology did make sense, initially, because it took an emancipatory form. The first household machines were large; they were a worthwhile investment for communal households, above all. The joy in such inventions was therefore not a joy in technology per se, but in the collectivizing potential of such technology. The large kitchen machine required a large communal kitchen; the centrally installed vacuum cleaner made life easier for all tenants, without discrimination—but once the large fan for it in the basement was no longer repaired, because the Hoover Company hoped to flood the market with expensive small vacuum cleaners, the poorer households returned to using a carpet beater, while the middle class expended all its energy for the next thirty years on equipping the home with the requisite electrical devices—an icebox, a floor polisher, a washing machine, a mixer, and a dishwasher—which at the time of their invention still swallowed up a slice of the family budget equivalent, in today's terms, to the cost of a mink coat or a car.

The good form concept came under fire after 1968 and was then quietly put aside. But the fact that the theory pursued back then is inadequate to the present era does not give us carte blanche to stop addressing either the device itself or the interrelation of technology and appearance manifest in it. The issue for us, rather, is to explore the nature of the clash between technological development and the philosophy of good form.

In the 1920s and '30s, it was believed that technology was nearing perfection and would gain in visual appeal. People imagined that the era of ugly technology, as epitomized by industrial-scale processes such as steel manufacture and railroads, was but a passing phase in which mankind had not yet completely mastered the laws of physics. In the 1920s, Ernst Jünger coined the term "workshop landscape" for this specific ugliness, which the "worker" of the era had to prove he was "man enough for" yet which was—apparently—already outdated, psychologically speaking.

These ideas are also at the root of the notion that technology overcomes its "technical" character by becoming organic. The use of heavy loads, extreme temperatures, and inordinate force was attributed to the fact that we cannot yet understand the subtleties of organic processes, which—so the opinion of the day—are triggered by catalysts unknown to us. However, such organic technology was at the same time bound to become more striking, given its perfection, because it would either clearly reference the laws of physics and so attain a consummate form, or come to resemble those organic forms familiar to us from the vegetal and animal realms.

The bicycle was a prime example of the first process, the combination of perfect technology and perfect symbolism. Hopes for the second process, an organic technology, were not fulfilled. Its remnants today are, on the one hand, utopian notions of proliferate synthetic structures [such as modular capsule homes], and on the other, realistic experiments in alternative agricultural production based, for example, on organic nutrient substrates and consummate zero-waste composting techniques.

Technology itself has failed twice over to take the predetermined path. It may have become more refined but not necessarily "smaller":

electronic controls are now used to handle heavier machines, higher temperatures, and larger plant than ever before. Processes of centralization continue and the apex of development is the nuclear power plant. — On the other hand, technology has not become more graphic in appearance. Semiconductor technology breaks down crucial processes and packs them plainly. Today, a normal technical device consists of a tangle of wires interconnecting other components that are obscure to the layman. Unless the casing of a device is clearly labeled, it is hard to distinguish a chemical gauge from a musical instrument; even the designer committed to making things fit for purpose has no choice but to hide such devices behind plain casing and properly label the consoles.

However, the idea of a technical function being easily decipherable was thwarted also by the fact that several optimal forms are feasible for most devices. Very few things are so very distinct as to clearly derive their optimal form from their purpose: again, only the bicycle springs to mind, besides such simple objects as a hammer or a pair of pliers. Most devices have a degree of complexity that makes several optimal solutions viable. Ideas about portraying the practical purpose of an object therefore flow into the design concept from the very start; the designer is free to modify the object in favor of a more functional form.

At the latest with the advent of Braun's electrical appliances, it became clear also in Germany that rival interpretations of modern style were in stiff competition, also in the world of good form. It was recognized that even forms supposed to be necessary on technical grounds would be supplanted by the vagaries of fashion. With hindsight it was acknowledged that this had been the case already in the 1930s, the legendary streamlined icebox being an early example of the rise and rapid obsolescence of technical forms.

This insight clarified once and for all that there was, conceptually speaking, precious little difference between forms that were fit for purpose and those found in popular, which is to say, market-oriented design. Design circles reacted to this lamentable discovery in two ways. The cynical ones among them elevated planned obsolescence to a goal of design, arguing that popularity, meaning marketability, is yet another feature of the technical product that the designer is obliged to create. — Others made a sacred mantra of the same theory: Marilyn Monroe is beautiful, the billboards of Las Vegas are beautiful, and popular design is beautiful; and anyone who denies this speaks in the name of an outdated, elitist ideal of taste. Why shouldn't we learn from the general public and, in so doing, give pleasure to the general public?

The theorists went even further. *Why* do these things please the public? And *why*, after a while, do they please it no longer? — Linguistics and semiotics pervaded design theory. Not the actual function of a product is at stake in design, but rather, the public's perception of that function. The product communicates something about its usefulness; and the content of this message ages, just as any communication does. This is why the look of the product must be altered, after a while.

An end to all these debates was preprogrammed, in a sense, once the youth revolt erupted in 1968. It is no accident that this elementary event—which is now part and parcel of our intellectual tradition and whose profound repercussions are denied only by those who have a bad memory and no longer recall how the world worked before 1968—it is no accident that this revolt began in the schools of architecture and design. For the youth revolt was about a new relationship between the meaning and the appearance of things; the look of an object was no longer to merely illustrate technical expediency or reproduce a pseudo-vintage design corrupted by the processes of capitalist production. What came to the fore, instead, was that an object embodies a specific historical moment plus the then prevailing social relations.

The youth revolt favors the *Sperrmüllstil*.[2] An object designed to satisfy elite tastes but then purged of its classist connotations by *Sperrmüll* recycling gives us a sense, if not of triumph over the repressive regime, then at least of the potential to assert our freedom in a predominantly capitalist world. All objects manufactured without submitting to commercial concerns give rise to this same feeling: this is what accounts for the success of the *Whole Earth Catalog* and its product list. Lastly, the products of foreign societies, particular those in the East, convey a sense of how people under different social conditions use different means to successfully manage their personal circumstances.

So, the youth revolt did not so much bring about a redesign, as a reinterpretation of the objects already in existence: their look is now read in terms of forms of organization. This brings us face to face again with the old adage that objects can be good or evil: they can authorize dependence, concentration, and repression, or they can keep us free of those. And this applies to both the production and the use of objects—Ivan Illich had merely to raise the veil, to put this insight into words: the *Tools for Conviviality* are diametrically opposed to all those products that foster loneliness and dependence.

And so, we may perhaps yet arrive at new criteria by which to judge devices. — Firstly, there is the demand for comprehensibility, which need not, however, go so far as that for the legibility of perfected technology. A product should be comprehensible to whoever has need of it; any parts it may contain that are not easily comprehensible, transistors and microcircuits, for example, should be integrated in the modular product as clearly identifiable and replaceable

2  From *Sperrmüll*, meaning bulky household objects put out on the street shortly before a scheduled extraordinary trash collection and often quickly gleaned by the public for recycling; and *Stil*: style.

parts. This brings us to our second demand, for repairability. It should be possible to repair a product without becoming dependent on centralized repair services. In particular, a product should not be thrown on the scrap heap because of a defective component that could be replaced. If and when the product or device reaches the end of its useful lifespan, it should be in a form that poses no harm to the environment. It should be made of a recyclable material or of one that breaks down without releasing toxins. Finally, the product should not directly entail the purchase of further products. It should both serve a purpose in its own right, and be freely combinable with other products that can be made at home or readily sourced on the open market. And what are the new criteria for design, you now ask? I could already name a few. Just imagine a new *Werkbund* commission striding around the *Mustermesse* design fair in Basel, seizing on an exhibited product, and asking:

- Is it made from raw materials obtained without oppressing anyone?
- Is it the product of meaningful labor that has not been divided into alienating steps?
- Does it have a variety of uses?
- Is it durable?
- In what condition is it thrown away, and what then becomes of it?
- Does it make the user dependent on centralized supplies or services, or can it be used anywhere?
- Does it privilege the user or does it inspire a sense of community?
- Is it a one-off purchase or does it necessarily entail further purchases?

## Design Is Invisible

Design objects? Of course, we can see them: the whole gamut of designs and devices, from a building to a can opener. The designer gives them a logical, ready-to-use form, premised on certain external parameters: in the case of the can opener, on the structure of a can. The designer of cans, for his part, considers how a can opener functions. That is his external parameter.

So, we can perceive the world as a realm of objects and divide these, for example, into houses, streets, traffic lights, kiosks, coffee makers, washing-up bowls, tableware, or table linen. Such classification is not without consequences: it leads namely to that concept of design which isolates a certain device—a coffee maker, say—acknowledges its external parameters, and sets itself the goal of making a better, or more attractive one; that is, of producing the type of thing likely to have been described in the 1950s as "good form."[3]

But we can divide the world up in other ways too—and, if I have understood *A Pattern Language* correctly, this is what Christopher Alexander strives to do. He does not isolate a house, a street, or a newsstand in order to perfect its design and construction; instead, he distinguishes an integral composite such as the street corner from other urban composites; for the newsstand thrives on the fact that my bus has not yet arrived, and so I buy a newspaper; and the bus happens to stop here because this is an intersection where passengers can change to other lines. "Street corner" simply tags a phenomenon which encompasses, above and beyond the visible dimension, elements of an organizational system comprised of bus routes, timetables, magazine sales, traffic light sequences, and so on.

3   See footnote 1 in Device and Form, p. 80.

This way of dividing up our environment triggers a design impulse, too, but one which takes the system's invisible components into account. What we need, perhaps, so that I won't miss my bus while scrabbling for change or because the newsagent is serving another customer, is a simplified method of paying for a newspaper. Some people instantly dream up a new invention—an automatic magazine dispenser with an electric hum—while we imagine intervening somehow in the system: selling magazines for a round sum, or introducing a subscription card which we can simply flash at the newsagent—in any case, some kind of ruling to tackle magazine distribution and that institution "the morning paper."

What are institutions? Let's forget Christopher Alexander's street corner in favor of that clearly identifiable institution, the hospital. What is a hospital? Well, a building with long corridors, polished floors, glossy white furniture, and little trolleys loaded with tableware for mealtimes.

This view of the hospital takes us back to the traditional design brief: the architect and the designer are called upon to plan hospitals with shorter corridors, more convivial atmospheres, and more practical trolleys. As everybody knows, however, hospitals are now bigger, their corridors longer, the catering service more anonymous, and patient care less caring. This is because neither the architect nor the designer was allowed to intervene in the institution itself, but only to improve existing designs and devices within set external parameters.

So, let's describe the hospital as an institution. Despite all its visible features, it is first and foremost a system of interpersonal relationships. Interpersonal systems are also designed and planned, in part by history and tradition yet also in response to the people alive today. When the Ministry of Health decrees that hospital catering is not the responsibility of medical staff but a management issue—or vice versa—this ruling is part and parcel of the institution's design.

The hospital owes its existence above all to the three traditional roles of doctor, nurse, and patient. The nurse's role evokes a myriad of associations, from the Virgin Mary through to Ingrid Bergman, and appears to be clear-cut. In reality it is far from clear-cut, as it incorporates a great number of more or less vital activities. The doctor, historically only a minor figure on the hospital stage, shot to the top in the nineteenth century on a wave of scientific claims swallowed whole with religious fervor and perpetuated to this day by TV and trashy novels, with the result that a formidable whiff of heart transplants now permeates even the most backwoods county hospital. And what about the patient? He has no role to play at all, you say? He simply falls ill, through no fault of his own? Come now, please make up your mind whether you want to be sick or healthy!—Evidently there is an element of choice in the matter. We can—and must—decide one way or the other, otherwise we will irritate our boss—our boss at work, or the hospital boss. A patient lies down—in Chodowiecki's day he used to sit—or ambles gratefully around the park, convalescing. He resigns himself in any case to the three-role spiel, although it has long been due for an overhaul; but more of that later.

Do other similar institutions exist? Yes, indeed: the night. Yet night is a natural phenomenon, you say? The sun is shining on the Antipodes and so it is dark in our neck of the woods? Anne Cauquelin was the first to posit that the night is artificial. And there is no disputing that human behavior shapes the night one way or another, in line with various man-made institutions. In Switzerland, I can work undisturbed after 9 p.m. then go to bed. To give someone a call at that hour is considered impolite. In Germany, my telephone is quiet all evening then springs to life at 11 p.m.—for the cheap-rate period begins at 10 p.m., whereupon all international lines are immediately overloaded, and it takes around an hour to get a connection.

Thus, the night, which evidently originally had something to do with the dark, is a man-made construct, comprised of opening hours, closing times, price scales, timetables, habits, and street lamps. The night, like the hospital, is in urgent need of redesign. Why does public transit cease to run at precisely the moment people drain their last glass in a wine bar, leaving them no option but to take the wheel of their car? Might not a rethink of opening hours make the streets safer for women obliged to return home on foot, late at night? Are we going to live to see the day, also in these climes, when car ownership is the sole guarantee of a measure of safety?

Let's take another institution, the private household. For the traditional designer, the household is a treasure trove of appliances clamoring to be planned. There are endless things here to invent or improve: coffee makers, food mixers, and dishwashers, to name only a few. The planner deploys novel means to ensure everything stays the same. Moves to reform the household were made around 1900: early mechanization fostered collectivization as well as untold experiments with canteens, public laundries, and centralized, built-in vacuum cleaners. Thanks to the invention of small motors, these amenities were reinstated later in the private household. Kitchen appliances save housewives' time, you say? Don't make me laugh!

The war on dirt is a subsystem within that institution, the private household. What is dirt? Why do we fight it? And where does it go after we emerge supposedly victorious? We all know the answer. We just don't like to admit it. The dirt we fight along with the detergents we use to do so is simply environmental pollution by another name. But dirt is unhygienic, you say, and who can avoid a spot of cleaning? Strange! Because people used to clean, even before they knew about hygiene. And besides, the filters used in vacuum cleaners are not fine enough to contain bacteria effectively. Which means that vacuum cleaners merely keep bacteria in circulation. What a shame for the vacuum cleaner, the designers' favorite brainchild!

Then how do people clean in hospitals, where hygiene is truly vital? Hygiene in hospitals rests, as far as I can see, on three pillars. The first pillar is purely symbolic—for sparkling white surfaces and the shine on polished (which is to say, wax-smeared) floors are considered the epitome of cleanliness. The second is antiseptics—toxins, in other words: an endless flow of new disinfectants designed to kill bacteria. Any success in these stakes is unfortunately short-lived however, for resistant strains never cease to develop and are selectively engendered, in fact, by these very toxins. And the third pillar is vacuum cleaning. In contrast to the domestic vacuum cleaner which releases dust back into the same room it was captured, hospitals' centralized air conditioning and vacuum-cleaning systems spread dangerous spores all over the place. Is there a solution to such unpropitious circumstances? Of course—but it falls neither in the designer's brief nor within his external parameters! The key to the problem is to redesign the health care system, above all by promoting decentralization.

Let's name one last institution: the production site. Much could be said on this topic but let us stick here to one sole point: workplaces—by which we mean jobs—are also man-made design objects. We're not talking here about making chairs at work more comfortable, or about cheering the place up a little with fresh wallpaper and a few potted plants. The object of design in this context is the particular task assigned to each individual laborer within the production process, and the degree of energy, knowledge, and skill, respectively of ignorance, boredom, or mindlessness he or she must invest to accomplish it. This applies not only to production sites in the narrower sense of the word, that is, to factory jobs, but also to administrative and clerical work. Workplaces—jobs—are designed ostensibly for productivity; yet productivity of a sort akin to counter-productivity. Automation, as it is called, destroys jobs which have hitherto been a source of satisfaction, while other jobs in the manual sector which could and should most urgently be rationalized remain unchanged. Here we can touch only briefly on the problem, without offering concrete evidence of our claim. Yet the main point is this: jobs, too, are designed, not only in the traditional sense of design, but also in the way the production process is broken down into various types of task which actively demand or render redundant the laborers' skill range and foster or hinder cooperation.

The previous comments were intended to show that design has an invisible component, namely an organizational-institutional dimension over which the designer always exercises a certain influence yet which, given that we classify our environment in terms of visible objects, tends to be overlooked. Insofar as the world is divided into object categories, and the invisible dimension acknowledged only marginally, as an external parameter, the world too is designed. Furthermore, institutions' resistance to change—especially given the wealth of technological objects now under development—is also a form of design: radiology equipment is designed for use by nurses in radiology.

In the following, we wish to consider whether these insights are of any use to us, or simply sad proof of the fact that the world is badly designed.

Whenever we think about design, we must address two phases: the phase of actual design or planning through to production; and the consumption phase, up to and including an object's disposal on the rubbish heap or in a museum. Let's take a look first at the established hypothesis on each.

On design: the objective is a functional object, whereby one might endlessly discuss whether functionality itself is identical with beauty, or whether the designer must add beauty as an extra.

And on consumption: technology and technical devices are neutral; their misuse stems from people's villainy. The *Werkbund Almanac* of 1914 featured warships as design objects while the journal *Werk* of

April 1976 described the cooling towers of nuclear power stations as an appealing venture for architects.

And now, two contrary viewpoints as a possible premise for a new way of describing the two processes, design and consumption:

On design: objects owe their form to the interactions inherent to the design process.

And on consumption: such objects in turn exert influence on social interaction; objects are not neutral; *Tools for Conviviality* exist (asserts Illich!), as do their opposite, objects which impede social interaction.

And let us test a third hypothesis while we are about it, a hypothesis on counter-productivity:

Every new invention which is put to use effects change and such change in turn necessitates new inventions. If all the problems which successively arise are dealt with conventionally, namely one by one, as isolated phenomena, the outcome is counter-productivity. Here is a brief example: a central heating system serving several apartments allegedly gave rise to the need to monitor each individual tenant's energy consumption. Gauges to measure the evaporation of liquid were installed and, as a result, each tenant now turns off his radiators whenever he goes out. However, each tenant also wants his apartment to be warm the minute he turns the radiators back on. Consequently, water in the heating system is kept at such a high temperature that even the thriftiest tenant ultimately pays more now for heating than when heating costs were split equally between tenants, without individual monitoring.

Let's begin, therefore, with the design process. Here, as we observed in our opening remarks, the designer classifies the world in terms of object categories rather than problem categories. This rests on linguistic determination, for to name a problem is simultaneously to identify the means—possibly an appliance—to solve it. When I complain that my electric onion chopper may indeed save me a moment's work but then takes ten minutes to clean, what springs to mind is not so much a return to the simple kitchen knife but a design for an appliance able to clean my onion chopper.

The objective, once named, becomes an instant solution, and supersedes any general endeavor on my part to cook more efficiently when time is short.

A further effect of this direct link between naming and the solution is the suppression of secondary considerations: with the exception of the appliance to be designed, no technical or organizational changes should be necessary. Whatever can be integrated in existing systems, however overloaded these may be, is considered successful: a waste disposal unit built into the sink drainage, an oven which self-cleans through pyrolysis, and so on. This type of troubleshooting has its roots in the designer's position within policymaking bodies: his job is to deliver ideas—but he bears zero liability.

In the late 1950s, the design school Hochschule für Gestaltung (HfG) in Ulm was the first professional institution to recognize that industrial design is counterproductive—yet the solutions it proposed were technocratic. They were based on a radical analysis of the desired outcome but failed to consider that outcome in its broader context. Students in Ulm were hence likely to submit papers which began something like this: "The exercise consists in raising 10 g to 20 g portions of semi-solid substances from a dish circa 30 cm in diameter then transferring them horizontally to an open mouth, whereupon a movement of the upper lip relieves the supporting structure of its load…" The result is not Charlie Chaplin's machine for eating but a fork with a modernist profile.

In the meantime, of course, it has been recognized that objects which have great symbolic value yet require only minimal inventiveness—tableware, for example—do not fall into the design field. Conversely, such things yet to be designed, or at the least their technical aspects, are too complex for designers. So, design must broaden its scope and embrace socio-design: a way of thinking about solving problems that results from coordinated changes made both to roles and to objects. One example may be to design a kitchen so inviting, it inspires the guests to help the host chop onions…

Before leaving the field of design to consider aspects of consumption, I want to slip in a comment or two on shopping and its "hidden persuaders." Of course, they have not yet thrown in the towel, those marketing and advertising professionals who sell depth-psychology soap powder as well as instant cake mix which is designed to make a mother feel she is breastfeeding the whole family. But the hype in the design field has pretty much died down: I now buy a new refrigerator when the old one breaks down, not simply because I want one with rounded contours. Rearguard action continues on the car market, however, where old-timers are a flourishing trade; and for other retail sectors the avant-garde has discovered the flea market. The flea market will be the place where dwindling numbers of the "use-once-and-discard" consumers meet the swelling ranks of postindustrial society.

This is not to say that progress, in its positive and its counter-productive guise, has ground to a halt. But the sector in which it is still being made is limited. Progress holds sway in production for the "white" [official] market but gray market trading, moonlighting, self-sufficiency, barter systems, and informal mutual backscratching are on the rise too. "White" trading is still scoring points also in these areas: DIY hobby products have slipped onto the shelves among the detergent battalions. Yet these might be fleeting epiphenomena on the road to greater self-sufficiency. Whether we should welcome all this wholeheartedly remains uncertain: it panders to lower middle-class aspirations and harbors a threat of social isolation; but perhaps a retrograde step or two is the price society must pay for a springboard to new realms of experience.

With regard to use and consumption, we wanted to point out that objects are not neutral. Is there any such a thing as evil objects?

Goods are harmful when they foster our dependence on systems that ultimately pillage our resources or desert us. Doubtless, we are all attached to such systems and thus, susceptible to extortion. However, we can still limit the extent of our addiction. We should avoid those objects which compel us to buy more accessories. We should distrust media which provide a one-way flow of information, even though we can no longer do without them. We should exercise restraint in buying and using any goods which isolate us. The car is a major case in point, especially as it tends also to foster inconsiderate behaviors in its user.

The car has destroyed not only our cities but also our society. We can commission as much research as we like as to why juvenile delinquency is on the rise, why more women are attacked, why districts are becoming derelict, or slums, or no-go areas by night. As long as the defense against motorized crime is a motorized police force, as long as the pedestrian is advised to use his car, the solution can be named without any need for further research: motorization based on private car ownership has abandoned the pedestrian populace to greater insecurity as well as to an increasingly uncompetitive mass transit system.

This leads to our last remark: on counter-productivity. We have already mentioned the example of monitoring heating costs. That is only a minor aspect of the outrageous counter-productivity of the central heating system, every failure of which has been countered by a new solution which subsequently proved to be a failure, to the point where we now use our electronically controlled, overheated and, in terms of air hygiene, unhealthy central heating system in devastatingly wasteful fashion, as a boiler; and the central heating system is being superseded now by an even greater evil: air conditioning. Counter-productivity, as we have said, arises when inventions are used in such a way as to cause a break in the overall system, a break which is patched up in turn by a further isolated invention.

The sum of these successor inventions equals the counter-productivity of the overall system.

To return to the car: since the average inner-city speed for cars has been lowered to match that of cyclists, or pedestrians even, automobile manufacturers are now pursuing research into the automobile's successor. And what are they developing? A car fitted with an additional gadget which allows the car to be steered to its destination by an electronic short-wave remote control system, whenever it enters the city limits. Or to return to the vacuum cleaner: since the public has grown aware that vacuum cleaners are all the more damaging, the more efficient they are, i.e, the more powerfully they can whizz bacteria through the filter, the industry is looking at a successor gadget—and guess what that may be? You're right: a vacuum cleaner with a built-in bacteria filter!

Invisible design. Today, this implies conventional design which is oblivious to its social impact. Yet it might also imply the design of tomorrow—design which consciously takes into account the invisible overall system comprised of objects and interpersonal relationships.

## Landscape Gardening, Too, Is Part of the Construction Industry

Anyone who builds must also ask: But what is in between the buildings? — In the city, there tends to be architecture in between the buildings, for architects have come up with the academic repertoire of steps and terraces, parterres and sidewalks, slabs and paving stones, plinths and monuments. Letting untamed nature run riot over a house is a fairly recent fashion, and one feasible in our climes only rarely, at best in the Highlands. In the North, however, a building may spring up directly on the moorland. The Classicist forerunner of this effect is the lawn lapping the very walls of a house; and not only Modernism lives off this, but also its illegitimate offspring, the speculative building. While once the symbol of the pastoral landscape, complete with grazing cattle, the lawn has meanwhile become both a commonplace set piece and a million-dollar business for gardeners; and, moreover, an occupation on which owners spend all their leisure.

Usually, the garden marks the distance of a house from its surroundings, and we are talking neither about ambitious architecture nor nature in its—real or pseudo—virgin state. We are well aware that the garden, too, has an architectural history of its own, clearly legible in stately buildings to a greater or lesser degree; and it only subtly colors the gardens of the middle classes and farmers. It is preferable, in everyday terms, to speak of types that coexist in sync: the farmer's garden, which the average citizen variously turns into a flower garden, a shrubbery, an orchard, or a kitchen garden; and, for the city, two further types of space well shaded by trees, namely those "parks" with trees that can be pruned (the horse chestnut, yew, and beech), and that which we recognize as the "Romantic garden," owing to its winding paths and plum-shaped lawns.

There has been no drastic stylistic overhaul of the middle-class garden. The inhabitants' degree of self-determination and DIY is too high for that. How a house looks barely changes, until it is refurbished once more; a garden requires constant care and attention, regardless of whether it is to stay the same or be altered. Middle-class gardens have thus been eclectic from the very start, if definable in style terms at all. It must be said that the decline of public parks and gardens has played its part in their present appearance.

Arguably the Romantic garden became the basic model of the urban garden, either public or private, for certain historical reasons in the nineteenth century. Although adapted to the—of course, small—urban lots, it was a variation on the English landscape garden, decked out with additional novelties from the decadent period, especially the ornamental flower bed, whose combination with the natural garden can be noted already in the work of Pückler-Muskau. This basic natural garden model enhanced by some eclectic elements proved sufficiently versatile to respond to the various twists and turns of style during the historicism of the *Gründerzeit* period in Germany (1871–1914). Over time, the pond moves onto the symmetrical axis and is given a fountain; presently, asymmetrical elements prevail; and the styles of the garden laid out in front of and behind the house, respectively, are usually reversed.

More difficult to explain is why the emancipation from historical models and ground plan specifications in architecture—first signs of which crept in at the turn of the century, before inspiring the modern style of flowing, open ground plan—why this emancipation led, in the case of gardens, to a more stringent regulation and architectonic planning. It is difficult to show that social factors were the cause; it was probably simply that people tired of the Romantic aesthetic. It seems paradoxical nonetheless, that straitjacketing the elements could be welcomed at the time as an emancipation.

Detailed examination of why the architectural garden style was considered more "progressive" than the landscape style, after 1900, brings to light incongruities that illuminate other parts of planning theory, too. The landscape garden in its Wilhelminian *(Gründerzeit)* form is "complete" and so no longer animates its owner to do anything more. The architectural garden, however, is unfinished and processual, thanks to its fixed framework: it also introduced the shrubbery, probably the most stimulating form of horticultural activity for any amateur. With the perennial flowering shrubbery—and its particular variation, the Alpine rock garden—the architectural garden once again paid tribute to blooms; for these featured in the *Gründerzeit* garden only in the foreground, as a flower bed, and in the landscape garden, not at all. In particular the passion with which gardeners and gardening critics with a social conscience advocated the new architectural style, after 1900, shows that any superficial equation of formal appearance and perfection or of landscape style and open-ended design does not tally.

Today, the large, symmetrically laid out parks of this period have grown rare. Little heed is paid now to the fact that they were once celebrated as social achievements, as spaces that an astutely calculating citizenry afforded itself with an eye to the future, whereas now they are regarded as a waste of space. What may be the reason?

The message that is demanded of a park or garden today is very much tied to the concept of "recreation." Now, such recreation in the park does not take place at the physical level; walking and sitting around there is physically no more tiring than it is in the office. Rather, recreation consists in the senses relaying some relaxing signals to the brain. And today, once again, it is precisely these signals or signs—of asymmetry, organic forms, or frequent change—that are associated, by and large, with "a semblance of nature." For past generations, quite other signs spelled out recreation—signs of orderliness, regular structure, a uniformity of elements, a panoramic view—

and of course, it is this re-evaluation of signs, this shift in what signifies recreational worth, which has caused the older parks and gardens to so rapidly lose in value. In private gardens or any other to which the owner had fast access, the layout was changed with or without the landscape gardener's advice. In the case of public parks and garden, the options were either radically new planning or—although increasingly rare—a museological approach. But whatever the change, the fact remains that set pieces from the architectural garden repertoire are repeatedly used on a small scale, in keeping with the eclecticism of all our contemporary landscape gardening.

The Federal Garden Shows held in Germany and, at far longer intervals, in Switzerland aspire to represent the current state of the gardening sector. We are not mistaken, therefore, in regarding them as symbols also of the decline of the art of gardening. The most useless hybrids are derived from the two prevailing styles, the "parks and gardens" style with its overfertilized flower beds, and the "Romantic style." We see "Romantic" field campaigns—modulations of the terrain—totally saturated with blooming battlefields, as well as flower beds laid out beneath an old tree's spreading branches, which is to say, exactly where we ourselves would gladly spend our summertime, but where flowers are doomed to a slow death. Or we see flower tubs set into the lawn, or a pond flanked by naturalistically planted banks of reeds and with the nozzle of a fountain sprouting from its center… Teachers much appreciate this wealth of examples of what *not* to do and I personally own box upon box of slides of them. At the Stuttgart Federal Garden Show of 1977, a bold innovation was proposed: a meadow full of native blooms extending into a mature grove of trees. The Swiss gardening magazine *Der Gartenbau* almost took this to mean the imminent demise of the gardening sector. Too prematurely: Stuttgart gardeners themselves made sure there was no future for this meadow. They mowed down the flowers even before it was sown. "It would never have worked anyhow," said a gardener we spoke to while he was mowing. "We'd never have managed to sweep the meadow free of leaf litter in wintertime."

Where, after such devastating comments, might we find signs of a renaissance in the art of gardening? For we do need an art of gardening, after all, whether we like the term or not; we live in cities, and have no choice but to seek respite in their unbuilt areas. In urban spaces, it is increasingly vital to create areas or facilities for different levels of outdoor recreation for different publics—for mothers and their children, independent children, young adults, walkers, idlers, and so forth. Sprawling urban expansion further requires that such accessible spaces be spread far and wide. So, we are in need of approaches that make such spaces functional, accessible, and durable, as well as beautiful. Not all uniformly beautiful, but rather, each in its own way.

We first see such signs at the two ends of the spectrum. The one extreme is the small garden, the tiny private garden such as Bernard Lassus has put back in the spotlight. What do those simple folk do, who lovingly make a park of their tiny plot of land? What is the aesthetic of the allotment garden? Can the gardener learn from these simple folk, as the architect did from Las Vegas? — And at the other end of the spectrum is the large scale, the wasteland. How can care be guaranteed here, when the areas to be tended grow ever more numerous and sprawling? Surely there must be lessons for us to learn not only from the allotment garden but also from the wasteland, the railroad embankment, the gap between buildings?

For the sake of brevity, let's call the small, private, almost excessively cultivated garden the "allotment garden." The essence of the allotment garden is that it conveys meaning. Often this meaning is clear to the owner alone, or solely following an explanation; often, not even then. But at least any passing observer can invest it with meaning. Bernard Lassus has tried to decipher these meanings: a number of allotment gardens he observed contain symbols of distance. The small size of the garden hints at a larger expanse. The most beautiful example is the front garden found by Lassus in northern France, in which a flower bed shaped like a ship lies between the house and the sidewalk. A garden gnome by the window looks out at the ship through a telescope—only four paces distant, and yet it symbolizes the vastness of the sea.

What is the message behind those gardens laid out by the contemporary landscape architect? He diligently shifts his props back and forth on the plan: interlocking paving stones, quartzite slabs, dry vegetation, imitation stream bed, kidney-shaped flowerbed, a forest-edge-type border of shrubs; all elements which once held meaning, but whose meaning has long since been lost. Meaning? — It's an issue our landscape architect would want nothing to do with; he has far too good taste for that.

So, let's learn from bad taste! The public garden cannot convey personal meaning to the same extent as the private one can; the city department of parks and gardens can on no account install garden gnomes, even if its own so-called works of art are not much grander. The problem lies precisely in the fact that the garden's information is addressed to an audience whose cultural premises differ, yet who would nevertheless like to find a meaning. Here, the "meaningful garden," as advocated by Bernard Lassus and, in a different way, by Ian Hamilton Finlay, seems to us to be a feasible approach. — First of all, the meaningful garden is rich inasmuch as it contains a variety of meanings, not all of which need to be read. Thus, in the same garden it will be possible, as Lassus puts it, "to play on the prairie, sow crops, identify plants, imitate the croaking of frogs, get lost in the woods, or, thanks to minimal portrayals of the legends of the region, to dream of the location's fabled past."

The meaningful garden must somehow relate to the people's art of gardening. Meanings are of use only to those who can interpret them. Thus, the landscape gardener initially works with familiar elements, but only those not yet worn out by routine use. He returns to the churchyards, the chapels on the pilgrims' routes, the hills of Calvary, and the grottoes in Lourdes, such as were created in the late nineteenth century. But he does not stop there: as soon as the passer-by realizes, again, that messages are being conveyed, he seeks to interpret other symbols, too. And here, a new opportunity opens up for modern art, which now no longer need be "set up" in isolated alienation on a swath of lawn in a park some place, but can create a space with meaning in and of itself. Thus, the inscribed stones laid out by Hamilton Finlay are not monuments in and of themselves, but only in connection with the garden context they are placed in.

Not every public garden can be a meaningful one. Such refuges of poetry must remain rare, lest they become vulgar, and lest they impose themselves on a public that does not want them. Thus, the certainly more meaningful trend in modern garden design begins at the other end, as stated above, with the wasteland. Its prophet is Louis Le Roy, and its dogma is not yet written, because it must remain undogmatic. The wasteland garden is equated—also by Le Roy himself—with the ecological garden; and rightly so, but only in part. Le Roy's gardens are ecological: they don't need fertilizer, they don't pollute the groundwater, they don't contain plants grown in greenhouses or by complicated procedures, and they give native fauna ample opportunity to reproduce. So, they are ecological, but are not designed to be ecological. They have nothing in common with the so-called eco-houses, in whose glazed sections complex botanical and microbiological processes are set in motion, to foster ecological cycles. In the case of Le Roy, ecology is an effect, so to speak, albeit a welcome one.

The wasteland garden is rooted in the idea of the plant society. Neither a single plant nor a bed of a single plant species is self-sustaining; each requires care. Plants in the wild always live in a plant society; a group of ten to fifteen plant species form a carpet, in which the participating species crop up at different yet regular intervals. So-called rare and precious species are also preserved in these plant societies: the Turk's cap lily, the daffodil, the lady's slipper—they are rare, because the plant societies preserving them have grown rare; within these, however, they are not endangered.

Thus, even on sites that are only partly suited to vegetation, plant societies form ground cover that is either stable or changes in a certain, foreseeable way. Hence, not individual plants, but plant societies are "the daily bread" of any thrifty and considerate gardener. Plant societies are also sources of information for a passer-by, even if he doesn't know it. They give him information about biological as well as social conditions: a certain plant society says whether the soil here is dry or moist, poor or fertile, sunny or cool. It also says something about whether the land is used or abandoned, walked on, grazed, or maintained in some way, as well as how long it has been in this condition. By reading the plant society, the walker learns whether or not the farmer expects to make a profit at a place, and can accordingly decide whether he might sit down there and light a little picnic fire. This information, however complex the facts underlying it, and however late the sociology of plants was developed as a science, is available to all of us, even if we do not always know it.

Plant societies have an aesthetic effect, too, as a result of these communicative powers. We can reproduce in our gardens the effects of naturally occurring plant societies or, if the soil is unsuitable, at least approximate them with other plants. The joy inspired by the edges of a forest, which signal that no harvest is expected and therefore no farmer will drive away the family stopping there to take a rest, can easily be simulated in our own patch of weeds—and, too, in the public domain, with little maintenance and no labels, as a means to invite the public to properly use the spot in question.

The style of garden developed by Louis Le Roy would thus first of all be a means of mastering the larger scale. Extensive areas can be laid out without the gardener worrying about who will maintain them later. They have the dual advantage of perpetuating themselves continuously, without care, and of producing surprises—such as the appearance and disappearance of plant species—and, moreover, they invite the public to lend a hand and bring about change.

This method must by no means be limited to large areas alone. On the contrary, it can be used to quickly transform typical urban sites, disused pits, abandoned building sites, embankments, and slag heaps into places of recreation. Admittedly, adolescents are the only age group to make use of such places, at first; the older generation finds the aesthetics of these wild gardens too strange. But that there is indeed an aesthetics and not mere chance and entropy is proved by the tale of the garden that Le Roy himself created around the medical students' living quarters in Louvain-la-Neuve. Comprising rubble and quarry-sourced plant societies, the wild garden so clearly signaled an anti-authoritarian stance as to be promptly razed by command of the bishops of Belgium, against the will of the medical students and under police protection.

# And the Landscape?

In his *Critique of Judgment,* Immanuel Kant ranks landscape gardening as the leading art form: for it satisfies to the utmost the demands he makes of art, namely to represent purposefulness yet without interest or, in other words, a disinterested purpose. A landscape garden is a slice of landscape that represents a form of cultivation whose yield, however, is without "interest," which is to say, that no claim is made to any return on the capital invested therein.

A landscape garden is accordingly a portrayal, a representation; and the painter Joshua Reynolds also advises his students not to take landscape gardens as models for their paintings. Because these, to use our terms, would then be portrayed portrayals, represented representations—and what, after all, does any landscape that is not a landscape garden represent? And how do we come to look at it, as if it were a work of art?

Landscape is an odd concept, and its ideological content has been given much thought, in particular by the geographer Gerhard Hard. He begins by asking why geographers assume they have a right to bundle together certain phenomena and declare them a landscape and then judge, on this basis, whether something is typical of a landscape or not. By his way of thinking, not only all kinds of natural features and man-made things, such as drilling towers, conveyors, and blast furnaces, but also miners in blue flat caps, returning home from their shift, "fit" the landscape of Germany's Ruhr region. And does that apply even to the director of the closed-down mine, who is writing today to curtail the tenancies of the few remaining residents of his miners' housing estate? — No, it certainly does not; at least that's what our geography teacher would say.

Thus, the concept of landscape is based on a tautology: we take whatever seems typical to be a characteristic of the landscape, and also derive from it our idea of what may or not take place in this landscape—and the widely held idea that the Ruhr region is probably Germany's most "typical" landscape is itself the result of a systematically constructed myth: the fertile area between the Ruhr and Emscher rivers underwent such rapid changes in the late nineteenth century, not only because of the coal there, but also for certain historical and technical reasons, among them policy on tariffs and customs duties; and the fact that these changes themselves came to be regarded as a nascent "landscape" is doubtless the result of nationalistic propaganda propelled in view of, and during, the World Wars by those appointed stalwarts of the principles of empire, which is to say, teachers; and under the present conditions of decline and a certain nostalgia for the age of the railroad, this entire house of cards virtually comes to seem real.

To think of landscape in this—geographic—sense requires some to-and-fro between its aesthetic and scientific description. The roots of the landscape lie in the arts, first in poetry and then in painting. The landscape is a construct, an image in the mind's eye, which enables us to make sense of the countless impressions we have of our environment, namely by filtering some of them out; and to construct landscape in this way is a city-person thing. Our ancestors lived off the countryside and so, for sure, their impressions were filtered in other ways: they saw berries and mushrooms, animals they could hunt, then later fruits, fields, firewood, and whatever else might be gathered in winter; and a patch of grass, overlooked by whoever had mown the slope. Landscape is, therefore, the image in the mind's eye of someone who is not out to make a buck from his environment.

The capacity to perceive landscape depends, therefore, on the construct in the mind's eye. This construct is the sum total of the "civilization" which every human being unconsciously soaks up and carries with him. There's no need to read Horace to find beauty in a flock of sheep gathered around a watering hole; calendars, dime novels, and cigarette ads paint a picture of the "charming place," and adults show it to their children on Sundays. Yet the *locus amoenus* (charming place) is composed of staffage such as poetry and landscape painting first assembled and put at our disposal two thousand years ago.

In the eighteenth century, England was gripped by a strange need to depict landscape in the landscape—for a very specific social reason. In England, an aristocrat lived off his country estates by selling food to the city. Most of the money he made this way was spent at his palatial London townhouse. In the seventeenth and eighteenth centuries, alongside this landed aristocracy, the moneyed aristocracy acquired similarly large fortunes in London. However, these fortunes were earned in the city. In order to keep up with the nobility, the moneyed aristocracy likewise acquired country estates; there, however, money was not earned, but spent. Country life on these estates was not for real but only a simulacrum. The English gardens are representations of landscapes used purposefully, but "without interest."

However, in order that no one mistake the representation for real agriculture, the simulacrum was modeled not on the English, but on the Roman landscape. In fact, not only English artists, but even English bankers—such as Robert Colt Hoare—went to Rome to study the Roman *campagna* and see how it might be depicted in the English landscape. The temples, aqueducts, and ruins of the English landscape garden served to highlight the landscape, to make it visible to those who as yet really had no idea what a landscape might be, since they had previously regarded land only in terms of "interest," which is to say, in terms of its agricultural yield. That nature was neither to be represented nor confused with landscape, ever, in the landscape garden, even one bereft later of its ruins, is made instantly clear in the text which launched the English garden in continental Europe, namely the eleventh letter in Book IV of Rousseau's novel *Julie; or, The New Héloise*. The passage is there for the reading: it begins with the description of how the Baron transformed his ornamental garden planted with pruned horse chestnuts into a kitchen garden that was to supply the local farmers with mulberry branches for the production of silk. And just when the reader begins to think that this is the new landscape park, the assembled guests enter through a small gate into the former kitchen garden… which has, however, meanwhile been transformed into an ornamental garden, where the fruit now runs riot and is maintained "without interest." And to prove that renouncing profit is a serious intent and nothing to do with this patch of land being worthless or left to lie fallow, the cost of converting the orchard into a kitchen garden for show alone is mentioned. By this time, as we can see, the continental aristocrat is already very bourgeois and does his sums with great care. Yet he is still noble enough to know that he is not producing nature here, but an illusion.

Our present interest in these ideas is prompted by the destruction that has swept great swaths of our landscape over the last one hundred years. People were declaring that the landscape must be protected from change as early as the turn of the nineteenth century. But how to protect the landscape, if it is not an external reality but simply a construct in our mind's eye? Do we have to return to the eighteenth century and represent the landscape in the landscape? — There are signs that this was attempted at times, in the latter half of the nineteenth century. Thun's panorama captured the landscape of a particular moment in a trompe l'oeil mural in a rotunda. A while later, in Interlaken one evening, during the tourist season, a small theater presented and explained a series of alpine landscapes painted on banners. All of these things are somewhat reminiscent of Goethe's "Triumph of Sensibility," about a prince who never travels without nature in his luggage.

Over time, nineteenth-century tourism successively consumed every last landscape of Europe, from the most charming to the least.

In Switzerland, this began with the lakes of the lowlands, Lake Zu-rich, Lake Biel, Lake Geneva, and above all, Lake Lucerne, which were frequented already in Goethe's day. The following generation went to the Jura, to the higher lakes of Thun and Brienz, and the alpine foothills. Decades later, the stage above the lakes, including the great waterfalls of Giessbach and Staubbach, was likewise van-quished; people now found themselves in the valleys of the actual Alps. The mountain passes lost their terrors and centers of alpine tourism sprang up. Was it possible to go higher? — There came the mountain railways and alpine club huts, and the wintertime, too, was claimed. By the turn of the twentieth century, Switzerland was wholly geared to tourism and wholly at risk of being depleted by tourism.

It was this which prompted the idea of completely preserving landscapes, or at the least, the Swiss landscape—an idea of its era, and so one presented, naturally, in natural-scientific terms. The min-iature "glacier garden" created by a Lucerne innkeeper was to find a worthy successor in the country's major feat in the Alps, the Swiss National Park.

The idea of halting activity completely in order to protect and preserve the landscape from tourism as well as from exploitation by farmers and hunters proved to be something of a scientific ex-periment: to gradually establish what was imagined to be the pri-mordial and pre-stabilized state of equilibrium of a location that was not yet, or no longer, disturbed by man. Now, as we know, and as experts are far better placed to tell us, no equilibrium of this sort was established. With or without human disruption—Is man actually a part of nature, or not?—instances of imbalance continue to occur, the most significant of which is the current concentration of deer in the National Park. It transpired, moreover, that certain phenomena considered to be the acme of naturalness depend on human economic practices: for example, beautiful alpine flowers do not thrive best on meadows protected from human footsteps, but on those where wild hay is harvested at least once a year. Thus, the question of landscape conservation is shaping up differently today. It is no longer: How do we protect the landscape from man? But rather: Who is still husbanding the landscape as we would wish? And this question inevitably begs another: What makes the landscape beautiful anyhow? For, as we saw at the start, the landscape is the sum not of all the phenomena surrounding us, but rather of those impressions selected because they convey to our senses the desired perception of landscape. So, if it is possible that not only medieval castles, but also mines and foundries become components of landscape, then perhaps, one day, the vestiges of derelict mountain railroads and ski lifts will be the object of nostalgic musings and the settings for memorable walks.

But if we assume, as seems highly likely, that people will continue for the time being to find beauty in traditional agriculture, which is to say, in that form of agriculture presently being supplanted by the rationalization of food production, then we must ask ourselves, how this beauty may be preserved. In all likelihood, areas of Europe will diverge ever more radically: one half is losing its beauty to monoculture. Owing to their uniform use, swaths of agricultural land are now aesthetically uninteresting or downright grim. In certain areas, animal husbandry has degenerated to the point where animals are no longer put out to pasture but are kept in sheds, while the former pastures serve only as a dumping ground for cattle manure in so concentrated form as to stop the grass from growing. — Other parts of Europe are being left to lie fallow, because farming them in a global market no longer seems economically viable.

If this prognosis is correct, if huge areas of land are indeed to be left lying fallow, then we need not worry about the rise of "national parks." But as we will see, nature left to its own devices in the lowlands triggers even more erratic and virulent cycles than it does up in the Alps. This fallow land will not be beautiful, will not even be accessible. If we want to keep the fallow land at least for leisure, it must be preserved, one way or another.

This is why today's landscape planners and designers are faced with more far-reaching problems than ever before. Preservation of the threatened landscapes can be achieved in two ways only, and probably the two must be combined: on the one hand, extremely extensive care by truly rational means, so as to maintain large areas in relatively balanced conditions; and on the other, usage on a hobby basis, whereby city people's appropriation of landscape for hunting, fishing, or grazing fosters interest in its preservation and thus protects fauna and flora from the all too drastic effects of change. It is alarming that the human activity devised to prevent destruction—sport—has now become an element of destruction. Sport was once a way for an urban society to carry out activities whose setting remained essentially unaltered, from start to finish. It was highly progressive, allowing masses of people to enjoy themselves without doing harm to the luxuriance and beauty of the environment. Today, sport—which in the Alps basically boils down to motor sports and skiing—has become a real menace to the landscape. Planning ski slopes incurs the removal of humus layers built up over centuries, and cutting routes through forests triggers processes that can never be reversed. — While landscape preservation in line with modern planning relies on popular support, it must take a stand against mass sports and other harmful types of use.

# Can the Townscape Be Preserved?

Compared to the mere protection of individual buildings of art-historical or historical value, the idea of preserving an *Ortsbild,* a townscape, or the look of a village, is a step forward in two respects. On the one hand, its preservation seeks to keep important objects in their natural environment and conserve a broader framework that suits these aesthetically, socially, and historically, and raises the overall value of the ensemble. On the other hand, the concept of a townscape does not preclude a certain transformation: its preservation does not require the place to be fossilized for all time in a former historical state, as our landmark preservation guidelines currently posit. Instead, certain criteria or dimensions of a place should be preserved, namely those that are the essential defining features of its appearance.

What does this townscape actually comprise? What is protected? Where are changes tolerable? — As suggested by the term "-scape" (or *-bild*, in German), what is to be preserved is the aesthetic impression evoked in our mind's eye by the preserved locality. A painted image consists of those elements that the painter deems essential to his message and thus incorporates in his work; likewise, an "image," figuratively speaking, connotes that sense of beauty arising from contemplation of a place. To a certain degree, we filter out any "non-essentials"; we generously overlook the tasteless beer advertisement at the historic inn, the insertion of a storefront window into the old farmhouse next door to it, a remnant of weather-beaten announcements pasted on the town hall facade, and a telephone booth plastered with posters. The sum of these disruptions is not enough to dispel from our mind's eye our image of a historical town.

The word "-scape" serves thus to express that some things may be missing from the location's once complete inventory and that others may indeed be altered, but only if we are then still able to grasp in full the former ensemble. This brings us to the practical matter of exactly how much may be missing, for this to work? Which changes can the townscape endure? When does disruption become so radical as to completely dispel the favorable associations hitherto evoked by the small town, for us and for others?

Before considering this question in more depth, we must touch on another point: the "-scape" of the town is not the same for all who see it. Just as ten painters paint ten different pictures of the same landscape, so, too, different viewers see different things in one and the same feature. Distinguishing what focuses our senses from what may be dismissed as "nonessential" is very much a personal matter. There are individual distinctions, distinctions that can be traced back to a person's education and interests, but above all, city people and farmers view the townscape very differently. And so, after our primary question—What constitutes the townscape?—the second one is: Whose image of a place do we preserve?

Or perhaps we must spell out that question more clearly: Who do we preserve the townscape for? The discovery that a small town is a *locus amoenus* (a charming place) was undoubtedly made by city folk who visited the countryside for pleasure and recreation. In the eighteenth and nineteenth centuries, when these city folk began discovering the charms of small-town life, the townspeople or villagers themselves were doubtless driven by quite other questions: Was it possible to live there, was the land fertile or rent free, and did the forest yield sufficient wood for the whole winter? These are important questions, and together they add up to the townscape. But the city folk found particular appeal precisely in those towns it was difficult to live in, the towns the farmers' sons were fleeing in droves. — And there was always one rural dweller or other who took a new aesthetic view of the surroundings, more akin to that of the urbanites. Nonetheless, it seems to us useful to recall, at this point, that the aesthetic approach to local construction issues represents an intervention by city dwellers in a country town's own affairs, and so is part of the city's domination of the countryside.

But to return now to our question of what makes a place "as pretty as a picture," and of what must be preserved in order to retain our sense of a *locus amoenus*. After negotiating the historicist viewpoint, according to which only the historically most important buildings must be preserved, and in total, the usual answer is usually this: essential aspects of the townscape are its spatial proportions, the size of squares, the width of streets, the height of houses, the siting of the town hall in relation to both the church and the market square, and where the farmhouses stand in all this; and these same spatial proportions must be preserved in the built volumes and voids. This well-established answer rests on an architectural tradition dating back to Camillo Sitte. Sitte was the first to translate the illogical proportions of medieval town squares into abstract ground plans, and to recommend that these be copied. As traditional as this method is, it suited the modernists very well, for they above all set great store by the effect of abstract proportions stripped of the ballast of the concrete building with its peculiarities and ornamentation. And it is possible still to this day to come upon a class of freshmen architecture students dispatched by their professor to a historical town center or village, for the sole purpose of investigating "the spatial" with a pencil and yardstick, which is to say, to gauge the effect of vacant volumes purged of their structures and decorative features.

These two traditions, the historicist one of restoring buildings true to history, and the urban design one of reducing them to spatial proportions, together comprise the now common theory and practice of townscape preservation. A townscape is best preserved by restoring the most outstanding buildings—the church, the town hall, the houses of major local families—to their *original* original condition (on which a brief word should be said), as well as by preserving the proportions and permissible heights of the rest of the prime building stock. — Our critical question must accordingly be: Will these elements impart a sense of "the townscape" to both us and our descendants?

We believe that before inquiring into the feasibility of townscape preservation, we should examine the question of what exactly comprises the charming townscape. We should examine it without fear of finding that the townscape perhaps cannot be handed down from one generation to the next, after all, and that socioeconomic changes in our small towns are destroying beyond repair those elements of which the townscape is composed.

Both the economy and the look of our old country towns and villages were shaped by agriculture. The changes they are undergoing reflect modern development of the agricultural sector and the ensuing reorientation of farmers to other professional fields. In brief, these events can be traced to the following factors. Agriculture is being rationalized; artificial fertilizers and farming equipment now enable an ever smaller number of people to produce an ever greater yield from the same land. But this rationalization goes hand in hand with a reduction in self-sufficiency: people no longer produce for their own household, but for the market. The agricultural sector is adapting to the division of labor and the market economy. These developments are leading in part to a concentration of agriculture: the smaller farmers are giving up, while the larger ones are buying up or leasing more land. In urban planning terms, this manifests as resettlement or rural sprawl: as a rule, it's the farms outside the country towns that tend to survive.

In social terms, this entire development is neither simple nor single-track. It changes family and social structures as well as the consciousness of the local population, agricultural and otherwise. In the course of this development, each locality goes through its own particular phases of crisis and prosperity. Yet there's a common problem, too, namely the shifts in rural values and ranking; since the success of farming is now likewise measured in money terms, it is just a job like any other; other professions (if successfully pursued) are consequently equal to it in status. This altered mindset also devalues objects of prestige in the farmers' everyday lives and holidays: the purebred herd; the horse-drawn cart used to deliver milk as well as to make an entrance at the village fair; the old farm and the beautiful kitchen garden: none of them is cost-effective.

Not that the country-loving urbanite has any business deploring this development as such. It was the urbanite who failed to protect Switzerland's beautiful cityscapes and centers from being steamrollered in the 1960s by service sector corporations and companies, so he of all people should now sympathize with the small country town, where a bank branch, small hotel, department store, and garage have sprung up on the main street and market square. Proportions in the towns, as in the cities, have been altered or even skewed beyond recognition. But would those townscapes in our mind's eye have remained intact, had these new developments always stuck to our customary local eaves heights and building depths? — Surely, no one could seriously think so. Proportions alone do not a townscape make.

And this brings us back to our question about criteria for the townscape. Places used to be shaped by their local economy, that is, by agriculture. Anyone who could read the signs would glean from the main street information about the proprietary and economic circumstances of its inhabitants and users. Volume and ornamentation are not the only signifiers in this flow of information. The types of information conveyed by usage are far too superficial to be reflected in the buildings, which is why they disappear into oblivion, lost forever more, once usage ceases.

Let's put ourselves in the shoes of a group of children who want to start playing at hide and seek on the high street. The era of asphalt has yet to arrive; the narrow side streets consist of a dual wheel track between downtrodden grass and plantain, and a hoof track in the middle. The high street itself is too busy to be overgrown, the tracks are smudged from all the swerving past one another, and the gravel makes an ideal playing field. However, some heaps of steaming horse manure alert the children to the fact that this is no place to begin a longer game; further traffic is sure to constantly interrupt them. But there are other places to play: here, on the driveways to the farms, lush plantain and chicory blur where the road ends and the farmyard begins—here, not even the so-called private property is "private"; traffic is allowed to swerve onto private land, just as the farmer, when he has too little space at harvesttime, has his wagons line up on the public road. The carpenter next door goes about things the exact same way; he has just bought timber and wastes no time asking whether it should be stored still in his yard or already on the common. There is another larger place that the children are now considering: the low vegetation and the border of nettles tell them that this spot is not currently in use and, therefore, no one will chase them off. On the other hand, the vegetation would be higher, were the spot never used at all; cattle shows are held there three times a year. Ball games would be allowed here, but what about making a fire? Finally, the children move on to the edge of town; here, a demolished house is now nothing but a high pile of rubble, its edges completely overgrown by thistles—a sure sign that no owner is interested in this property at the moment, and a small fire is therefore permissible.

This small sketch is intended to show that the look of the traditional village or small country town is composed of information directly related to usage. The characteristics which betray signs of such usage are by no means only architectural in nature; rather, this village or "townscape" is reflected also in road surfaces and their deterioration, and above all in incorrigible spontaneous vegetation, so-called weeds, which, whether we are conscious of it or not, reveal to us in the most precise detail, how, and how often, and for what purpose a spot has been or continues to be used.

Let's walk through the same small town today, in the age of the automobile, the monoculture, and townscape beautification. The farmers along the main street have largely disappeared, and anyone who does still farm hides behind the house any signs of his shrunken operation. The land between the road and the house no longer serves a purpose, so is divided up among the owners: a surveyor determined the extent of the road and the common land, the "Allmend," as well as where private property begins. The town council then had a stone curb set along this line.

Where common land extends along the roadside, the town council has created leisure spots: stone benches alternate with beds of begonia and geranium. The town fountain, too, has been moved from the center of the street to a niche, and surrounded by flowers—the geraniums leave a discreet gap for the "Do Not Drink" sign. Residents of the main street now find themselves suddenly in possession of a space that has no function, extending from their own house to the said stone curb. A traveling salesman in artificial stone pavers was the first to espy an opening: hence, most townspeople now have not only a paved driveway, but also a row of parking spaces for themselves and their fictitious guests. A nursery owner must have been the second to arrive, because the rest of the space has been turned into a garden in line with the latest urban taste: clusters of cotoneaster, barberry, juniper, sumac, and other dry shrubs of that sort. Lawn will be sown on the remaining square meters; the purchase of a lawn mower per household is now imperative.

Enough: it is not our intention to mock. We are merely asking: What comprises the townscape? What information does this place relay to our brains? Even if, say, we assume that no building has been demolished or remodeled, this townscape has changed completely. However, the changes affect nothing of that which the townscape historic preservation authority deems "essential": neither proportions, nor open spaces, nor built volumes. Some patches of weed, chicory, nettles, grasses, and thistles have disappeared; and in their place are flowers and bushes and the inevitable interlocking pavers. That which has changed, however, is our sense of place, for the sum of the information we derive from all these small details is now entirely new.

What conclusions can we draw from these deliberations? Must we resign ourselves to the fact that the townscape is something impossible to preserve? What does all of this now mean, with regard to townscape preservation? — It means that restoring buildings and preserving volumes and proportions may well be worthwhile, but it will not suffice to preserve for the future the look of the place as it once was.

The changes brought about by economic restructuring—and not least the well-intentioned refurbishment schemes themselves—affect so many of the seemingly incidental yet in reality defining features of a place as to radically alter the overall impression

But how can we influence the sum of these image-defining features? — To begin with, we must acknowledge that economic restructuring is well underway. It is impossible to artificially reproduce the traces of former usage. On the other hand, there is no need to accelerate development in areas where it has not yet taken off under its own steam. Many a requisite refurbishment or monument preservation is accompanied by horticultural interventions that an urbanite evidently had a hand in. This is to be avoided. Furthermore, an eye for temperate design should be schooled in the small towns themselves, and among those responsible for the towns' new image, so that the unique peculiarities of the place may be preserved and highlighted. Not every open area should be covered with interlocking pavers, not every redundant wagon wheel be displayed in the front garden, not every old trough be filled with begonias... And as for the leisure spots, with their fountains and benches: village structures are not yet of a sort that villagers care to be seen as idling tourists; therefore, these new facilities are not used, for the most part, and so look doubly out of place. — Surely, it must be possible to raise a little awareness among the people themselves and among the local authorities about what would be beautiful and fitting for a place in its present state of development, even if the brochures of the building suppliers, seed stores, and paint factories conjure an altogether different image?

## The Minimal Intervention

Criticism of planning drives the established experts to exclaim in desperation that, probably, it is safest to do nothing at all, because only then do we make no mistakes. They believe that such a claim is rhetorical, and that their interlocutor will immediately correct it by saying that's not what he meant, because of course something must be built.

But we believe, we have provided in this book ample evidence of the fact that the social mechanisms in decision-making tend to culminate in buildings, also in cases where softer strategies would be more effective.

We are in search of a theory of planning and the name we have given it, "the minimal intervention," underscores our premise: that every issue should be mitigated strategically, by means of intervening in it as little as possible, for this alone serves to minimize the unexpected and harmful consequences. In the past, the need for austerity was a regulatory factor that worked to some extent in favor of the minimal intervention. Since our decision-making mechanisms date from an era of limited resources, we, as a society, assume that the interventions we decide on are also the most minimal ones possible. But this has long since ceased to be the case: although society's resources are limited even now, a very substantial proportion of the public budget is constantly earmarked for construction projects which even interventions by the planning authority fail to steer, with the result that more than necessary is being built, all the time.

The most minimal intervention of all is to prevent construction, and today, this is without a doubt a major political concern and the only one that can actually rally popular support. While, in the following, the attempt at a theory of minimal intervention begins with an aesthetically founded concept, it must be pointed out immediately that, for both economic and ecological reasons, the concrete prevention of construction is of paramount importance to the present author. He counts his part in preventing a supermarket being built on Basel's market square among his most gratifying triumphs.

The French garden designer Bernard Lassus once stated in an interview—in reference to criticism of academic landscape design—that the need to intervene in the landscape is rooted first and foremost in people's failure to recognize as landscape all that already exists around them; anyone hoping to create a new landscape fails to see that a landscape is inevitably already there—in particular, designers of Germany's Federal Garden Show *(Bundesgartenschau)* often claim that they have created a landscape in some place where previously "there was nothing." Therefore, the minimal intervention consists first of all in understanding the aesthetics of the existing situation.

A prime example of my point is the wetlands "created" along the River Fulda in Kassel by the Federal Garden Show of 1981. The Kassel basin owes its scenic beauty to the fact that the Fulda floodplain is ringed by hills, by the Habicht and Kaufunger forests, and so forth, which together delimit an area some 10 km in diameter. The beauty of the Fulda floodplain was discovered early on by the court of Jérôme Bonaparte, who held his pleasure parties there, and it continued to be enjoyed throughout the Romantic period, with boat trips on the Fulda. Then, firstly, the decline in agricultural exploitation and secondly, the tail end of industrial activity, in particular the excavation of gravel from the riverbed, led the Fulda floodplain to become semi-deserted and overgrown, factors which were by no means unwelcome among the locals. On weekends, families would go the floodplain for games and picnics, or to canoe on the dead arms of the Fulda; the reed banks offered opportunities for botanical inquiry, and the vestiges of barges and industrial plant, a Robinson

Crusoe-style adventure playground, while the ban on bathing in the old quarry lake was merely a further incitement to do so; and finally, the wealth of species to be found in this transitional vegetation was a sight that neither man-made gardens nor so-called natural biotopes could ever offer.

This is precisely the sort of landscape which is "nothing" in the eyes of the landscape designer. Since no one has explained to him the vital connection between the Fulda floodplain and the nearby ring of hills, he considers the former a non-event. A million cubic meters of earth have been moved around on this landscape: the dredged lake and the dead arms of the Fulda were converted into a kidney-shaped pond and artificial hills were built from any masses of earth not required for highway construction.

It is typical of the compositional talent of those landscape designers who operate from behind their desks that the numerous panoramic spots defined as such by the installation of a bench actually clash terribly with the landscape beyond them: either the nearby hills block out the line of the Kaufunger Forest on the horizon, or a factory chimney or high-rise building protrudes grotesquely from behind a hill, or spews its plumes of smoke from a hilltop, volcano style. In the sightline of an artificial river valley, designed for painterly effect, lies nothing less than the remains of a slag heap, for which evidently no use could be found… As for the vegetation, it has been diminished, as usual, insofar as the site conditions created by the gardeners—and perhaps even the gardeners themselves count as site conditions—considerably narrow down the relative wealth of species found on the uncultivated margins of a city. Finally, it must be noted that the cost of maintaining the Fulda floodplain, now that the Federal Garden Show is over, has been found to be so high as to require the Kassel Department of Parks and Gardens to close down the city's botanical garden, in order to prevent the deterioration of the "newly created landscape."

Therefore, the "minimal intervention," in this case, should have been to describe the long existent landscape in a way such as to render it visible also to experts and politicians who are blinkered by routine. This is no easy matter, because the idea of change so fascinates people that even those members of the general public who mostly used to benefit from the pre-development landscape and must have experienced the change quasi as a disciplinary measure are enthused by the concept of a "newly created landscape." Thankfully, a basic grasp of landscape seems still to be core to geography and natural history lessons, for it was schoolchildren, above all, who took an interest in critiques of the 1981 Federal Garden Show.

Accordingly, a first step towards minimal intervention might be either to open the viewer's eyes to the existent landscape or urban situation, or to hone his present awareness of it. The frame of reference for all things charming is so broad, in our civilization, that even extreme landscape forms can be subsumed in it, if only they are explained. The minimal intervention would go a step further, were it not only to rouse, but also to alter, the viewer's willingness to see. We cite below a number of examples of contemporary artists or landscape designers who change the meaning of the existent landscape by intervening, not in the landscape itself, but in the viewer's imagination. The minimal intervention, in this case, is semiotic insofar as it offers a sign or a signal.

In many places the authorities themselves have already unknowingly made use of the minimal intervention. A hiker who comes suddenly upon a wayside sign announcing "Nature Reserve" sees the landscape around him with fresh eyes from that moment on: the tree, the flowering plant, the circling bird of prey are instantly perceived in the light of their beauty, their worthiness of protection, and their naturalness. — The English gardener Ian Hamilton Finlay applies this principle in his art. His garden in Scotland, which is modeled on the traditional landscape park, contains inscriptions in stone or wood which effect a shift in the viewer's consciousness of whatever his eyes behold. Finding the words "See POUSSIN Hear LORRAIN" on a Scottish moor lends a new dimension to his outlook, for the place thus rendered special illuminates the history of landscape painting. A stone set besides a tussock and bearing the letters AD, Albrecht Dürer's initials, invites us to regard said tussock from the perspective of a painter still wavering indecisively between art and the study of nature. Hamilton Finlay's work is thus undoubtedly an essential building block for the aesthetic aspect of the minimal intervention theory as a planning method.

These thoughts may all be very subtle and oriented solely to aesthetics; a planning theory of minimal intervention they are not—yet. Whenever actual interventions are planned, (and such planning is in keeping with "the minimal intervention"), we must presume they are exceptional. The usual intervention, which we regard as too big and too brutal, is a child of routine. It is planned by people who learned to plan from teachers who believe in the universal applicability of rules. What once proved (or not) to be a "neat solution" for one place is reapplied, wholesale, to a different place altogether. Since the state and urban planning professionals both scorn to monitor success, routine perpetuates itself as an apparently successful course of action.

The idea of the minimal intervention arose during a series of visits we made to Belice, an area of Sicily struck by the earthquake of 1968. In German-language newspapers and even in Italian ones, it is persistently claimed that while money was collected for the victims of the earthquake, nothing was ever done; the Mafia must have pocketed all the funds. Nothing could be further from the truth—unless the construction industry is to be taken for a Mafia. For huge and costly interventions have indeed been made throughout the Belice region, which before the earthquake was a fertile but totally impoverished zone. The Ministry of Planning in Rome meant to do some good in Belice; but the question remains as to whether the size of an intervention is a guarantee of sizable success.

The first intervention was, how could it be otherwise, the construction of a highway from Castellammare del Golfo to Vallo di Mazara. For anyone obliged to travel this route from end to end, it has greatly eased traffic conditions. For the local people, who have to cross the valley to go from their home to the fields and back again, it poses an obstacle. Even if cars are still so rare as to allow the locals to occasionally risk crossing the highway by mule, median strips and guardrails are a considerable hindrance to handcarts. For north-south travel in the valley, a suitable and cheap means of transport had long been at hand: the railroad. Evidently, the new plans were laid in such a way that the railroad no longer stands a chance. Neither were the reconstructed villages allotted to the railroad stations, nor the rebuilt railroad stations to the new villages. Vicious rumors have it that the recently rebuilt station at Calatafimi sells, on average, three tickets a year. The planners behind the reconstruction of Gibellina could have seized the opportunity to assure the town a better rail connection than the old station at Salemi, which is now still its closest one; but they want to sell cars, not train tickets.

The towns of the Belice region provide abundant evidence of the planning errors common to professional interventions. For the small town of Partanna, which has circa seven thousand inhabitants, the planners planned a highway intersection with a footprint equivalent to one-third of that of the town overall. It is possible to access the highway from all over town or to leave the highway for any of the small town's streets, without ever stopping at an intersection. In 1980, students drew up plans to show that the entire population of Partanna to have suffered damages from the earthquake could have been housed on the area covered by this highway access road.

The town of Calatafimi demonstrates a further error of professional planning: the superstition, namely, that infrastructure creates structure or, in other words, that if roads are built, private initiatives will take care of developing housing and jobs. It does look really rather ghostly, when an entire town consists solely of streets, parking lots, sidewalks, and traffic lights, while vacant lots stand there, undeveloped.

However, the road network that constitutes Calatafimi and likewise the reconstructed town of Gibellina are also symbols of faith in the universal applicability of model solutions. It is not uncommon for a planner to think that the English new town model will be perfect for the resettlement of Sicilian farmers and workers. That the climate is perhaps quite different, that it's difficult to cross open squares under the summer sun, that not everyone owns a car, even today, and that community life unfolds along completely different lines are subtleties that the planner hears nothing of, in the course of his higher education.

The streets of Gibellina are allotted to various forms of traffic: the "front" doors of each row of houses give onto a pedestrian street, and the rear doors, onto a garden zone, which in turn gives onto a road for vehicle traffic. The planner assumed that the pedestrian streets would be a place for adults to mingle and for children to play, whereas the non-pedestrian roads would assure delivery of goods and access for care of the gardens. But how does a farmer or an artisan get home in the evening? — By the very route that the planner correctly foresaw as the "rear" entrance; he puts his tools in the shed, his mule or car in the garage, and then plods with heavy steps through the kitchen garden into the kitchen. And where do the children hang out? Do they stay out front, where there is nothing to see? Are they not far likelier to be on the side where an occasional vehicle or a mule, the neighbor, or even their father himself can be expected at any moment?

In fact, the planners of Gibellina were obliged to note that the residents do not open the "main entrance" of their house. The pedestrian streets are unused to the point where street lighting there is no longer considered necessary; it merely disturbs people's sleep.

The houses that were built on private initiative have a floor plan skewed by 180 degrees: their "front" door faces the vehicle access road. The mayor is seriously considering tearing out the paving on the pedestrian streets and offering them to residents as gardens.

Planners are rarely at a loss for an excuse. The planners of Gibellina can present their blunder as a pleasing manifestation of the will of the people: with a patronizing pat on the back, they permit people to grow tomatoes, where actually pedestrian traffic was intended; after all, participation is all the rage. The planners do not have to replace the fertile Sicilian soil that was lost due to their mistaken planning. And it means equally little to them that the residents make a living largely by carrying out the planners' nonsensical plans; where the many construction workers are supposed to work once reconstruction is complete, and who will inhabit the cities once they leave, remains a mystery.

The idea of the minimal intervention is closely tied up with rejection of the one-size-fits-all type of experience. Experience is not about how we once successfully pushed through an intervention, in spite of resistance. Rather, the fruits of experience should be to demonstrate clearly, in each particular situation, how to obtain the information that will enable us to appropriately tackle said particular situation, precisely.

# The Minimal Intervention (1982)

The press is still churning out its same tired mantra: reconstruction of the Sicilian towns destroyed by the earthquake of 1968 will be a long time coming, for the Mafia has long since pocketed the funds donated to this end. Anyone visiting the Belice finds another picture altogether. A brand-new highway, on which traffic is admittedly still light, has now opened up the entire region. The earthquake-damaged towns have acquired new neighborhoods fresh from the drawing boards of academic urban planning departments. Some of them are already inhabited—the town of Gibellina, for example, which is modeled on an English new town—while other projects, such as the new districts of Calatafimi, another instance of academic urban planning, have not yet progressed beyond the road building stage; likewise, the highway intersection at Partanna: the road builders have used a town of only a few thousand inhabitants to demonstrate how a metropolitan road network should be linked with a highway.

Belice's "earthquake valley" was therefore the perfect place to hold a seminar on "the minimal intervention," the aim of which was to tackle aspects of a new theory of planning. This seminar was the third in the "Talks on Parks" series organized by the earthquake-damaged town of Gibellina. The series was Gibellina's endeavor to raise awareness of problems impending since the open spaces in this "English" new town were laid out far too large for the scorching days of summer in a small Sicilian town, as well as a contribution to a supra-regional cultural program in collaboration with the University of Palermo.

So, we were in search of a theory of minimal intervention, and adopting a variety of approaches was to help us devise it. Some lectures from the field of critical urban planning highlighted the irreversible consequences of centralized intervention in locally determined situations. Other lectures pursued the seminar's aim by addressing landscape design, inquiring into whether it is the simultaneous use of contradictory motifs from the repertoire of academic routine that is currently destroying the capacity of garden design to put across any message at all. Finally, speakers tackled how history is destroyed and visualized, which is an especially important topic in a new town rebuilt 18 km away from the razed town

Common to all these approaches was the awareness that man lives in environments that are partly visible and partly invisible. Therefore, physical interventions in the world bring incalculable shifts in consciousness in their wake, which in turn may provoke the need for more planned demolition.

From the traditional planning viewpoint, the theory of minimal intervention is an aberrant drift into spontaneity: the profession remains stuck in its old routine. Nor can any help be expected from the official art circles currently retreating into the "true realm of artistic activity"… Nevertheless, the debate about minimal intervention as a byword of modern planning and design is at the vanguard. Easiest of all is to define our standpoint as the antithesis of that of our opponent. The theory of minimal intervention criticizes the aesthetics of academic planning's "neat solution": the planners' guild works with the one-off intervention that delivers the perfect solution. Moreover, such solutions are supposed to be exemplary and universally applicable: professional training for planners teaches solutions, not how to devise solutions. In psychological terms, the aesthetics of the neat solution corresponds to the puerile notion that reality can be fundamentally grasped by recourse to simplified models, and that solutions tested on models can be seamlessly transferred to reality. Forgotten is the fact that our understanding is always based on a reduced image of reality and that we are therefore unable, in principle, to estimate all the consequences of the consequences of our interventions. All too tempting is the puerile bliss in understanding and resolving reality with a one-stop cure.

Our second approach, as we have mentioned, was to examine the minimal intervention in terms of landscape, and thus also to critique the very concept of landscape. Our way of describing our entire environment as "landscape" is an ideological ploy. We thereby categorize the objects in our environment as typical or atypical: for example, the farm laborers at work in a field beneath the blazing sun are typical of the picturesque landscape, whereas the car parked by a realtor in front of a farm is regarded as alien to the landscape. So, the concept of landscape gives us a handy pair of glasses that obscures the true processes of landscape destruction and deludes us into thinking that it is possible to produce beautiful landscapes.

The fact that the destruction and reconstruction of a place can provoke in its inhabitants a sense of alienation and the loss of identity is no secret, nowadays, even among conservative planners. Objects that served in people's earlier everyday lives to anchor their sense of self are absent in the new environment. The latest architecture believes it can compensate this absence by citing other styles. Yet it is impossible to foresee which associations these citations will evoke in which persons, or whether a sense of familiarity would be better fostered by quite other complexes of visual and social signifiers. In any case, the minimal intervention is never about merely pasting a sign of the earlier existence onto the facade of the new one; its aim, rather, is to handle with care the everyday life and standard of living of the people affected by our planning.

A report on a town pursuing a policy of minimal intervention was delivered by Federico Oliva, the director of construction in the said town, Pavia. It has resolved to no longer plan for the year 2000 and for the inhabitants who will have moved there by then—which is to say, to plan no longer on behalf of the housing construction companies but, rather, for the people resident in Pavia right now.

Consequently, all planning is conceived as a careful, processual transition from one existing state of affairs to the next. Nothing hitherto of significance is to be destroyed by such transition, unnecessarily. If intervention does prove necessary, the proviso is to protect to the utmost whatever already exists. As for the way to deal with a landscape which must be altered to accommodate new developments or owing to shifts in the agricultural economy, nothing sums it up more clearly than the zoning plan of the town of Pavia itself, which states: "Why, for example, regard an area under planning as a tabula rasa, where the whims of a purely formal quest can be given free rein, although the land is dotted not only with farms whose preservation is required by the development plan, but also with terracing, groves, modest beaten tracks, drainage channels, and the rudiments of an extremely valuable urban or farming landscape? Why claim to invent a settlement, ex novo, on a blank sheet of paper, only then to breathe life into it by artificially reintroducing terracing, planting groves of trees, laying out footpaths, and even filling a small lake with water, which destroys the original rudiments of landscape and creates others that will be hard put to look equally charming? ... Moreover, we know from experience that all these new settlements that deny what went before them—however worthy the individual project—are of necessity built in stages, and that before they reach the desired end state, (if ever they do), they stand around for years, unfinished, cold, and lacking in expression, since alone their completion lends them character, warmth, and meaning."

The reflections of the English literary critic Stephen Bann take a far more abstract turn. For him, the minimal intervention is tied up with the mythical reading of landscape, whereby pre-existing meanings are invoked and a poetic landscape is created, without any need for the modern-day feats of the gardener—whose professional routine now includes transplanting mature trees. The model here is Chinese landscape painting, which, by striving to sublate antagonisms in the landscape, renders it familiar, so enabling us to identify with it. Western artists preoccupied with land art, however, can no more offer an experience of the minimal intervention than modern architecture with its citations. They far too readily content themselves with the traditional techniques of occidental design: perspective, geometry, and abstraction.

The French artist and landscape designer Bernard Lassus posits that intervention in the landscape initially ensues from a failure to understand what is already present. Anyone who replaces one image of the landscape with another must consider what we lose and what we gain by intervening. The garden architect's astounded defense "there was nothing there, before!" is no longer tenable. Anyone who designs a landscape must consider whether the meaning he is creating is of the sort to be understood by other people, also those with other cultural backgrounds than his own. In our pluralist society, a design must be open to multiple interpretations: one and the same park must mean other things for children than for the adults who accompany them. The landscape designer working in suburban zones should not only aim for harmony, but also design landscapes with critical import. Merely green-screening, to hide things away—which is what gardeners are obliged to do today—renders our everyday environment illegible, for it blandly merges incompatible objects in a continuum.

The opinion of the German vegetation expert Karl Heinrich Hülbusch is that any intervention in the form of gardening produces weeds. The relentless weeding, to say nothing of the use of toxins, which we are obliged to witness in our urban parks and gardens is a consequence of an aesthetic shift which leads us to see all spontaneous vegetation in the city as weeds. This happens because of the industrial nature of today's market in flowering plants. The flowerbed, a basic element of academic landscape design, imitates the vegetable patch, which must be rid of weeds, if we hope to reap a harvest.

So, the theory of minimal intervention holds that a plant may not be declared a weed just because ornamental gardening has degenerated into a flower factory.

Finally, Bazon Brock addressed the preservation of our historical environment by asserting that rubble and ruins must remain signifiers in everyday life. To illustrate the potential of ruins, he offered a historical interpretation of a situation in Berlin, namely a site flanked on one side by the Berlin Wall. The uninformed passer-by could never guess that a similar wall stood on this spot as early as the eighteenth century, enclosing a barracks in which the Prussian rulers imprisoned their reluctantly conscripted soldiers until allegiance had been knocked into them, to use the jargon of the day. They also shot deserters, at the time. The most minimal intervention of all, then, is to hone awareness of that continuity of circumstance which looks to us like—or is specifically showcased as—a one-off glitch that could be easily ironed out by a rational intervention.

If the ruin is an especially potent signifier of information that enables us to process the present, the theory of minimal intervention must concern itself with the construction of ruins. Whatever is unfinished or already ruinous is the antithesis of those "neat solutions" that, since always orthodox and always ending in disaster, destroy our world.

# The Minimal Intervention (1987)

An "unpainted landscape" is the landscape in our mind's eye, one we have composed by means of education and reading, and which allows us to perceive all that surrounds us as a landscape and to imbue it with meaning. The minimal intervention would be one that changes a landscape, not by using bulldozers and artificial fertilizers, but simply by changing the unpainted landscape we hold onto as a concept; for this alone leads us to read a different meaning into the landscape we behold.

There are two processes that contribute to forging our idea of the landscape: the secular process of our civilization—our cultural context—and the process of personal upbringing and education, which must echo the civilizing process, in much the same way as the embryo goes through past stages of phylogenetic development.

This cultural process begins when the city dweller, freed from daily labor in the fields, develops a new aesthetic awareness of the landscape surrounding his city. This relatively new perception of cultivated fields as landscape has become so commonplace that we have trouble even imagining that it may once have been otherwise. But even today, when crossing the Alps in a railroad car carrying tourists and farmers, we are likely to see foreign urbanites gazing through the windows and praising the beauty of the landscape, while the farmers say to one another, "I wouldn't want to be a farmer here; it's far too steep to mow, and the grass looks quite poor."

In his poem "The Walk," Friedrich Schiller suggests that this new aesthetic consciousness is a result of liberation from the material conditions of agricultural labor. The city dweller out on a walk sees "the happy people of the fields, not yet awakened to freedom" as a part of the landscape. He himself, who has gained this consciousness and therefore regards the landscape as a place of leisure as well as of work, becomes a spectator. In similar fashion, the geography teacher drilled into us the landscape of the Ruhr region: smoking chimneys, winding towers, and the miners in blue caps, returning home from their shifts, were its typical features. Happy people…!

So, as we see, the word landscape is tricky. On the one hand, we construct a coherent image from the myriad of impressions that affect us. On the other hand, we simultaneously draw lines between the typical and the atypical: coal mines for the Ruhr region, sheep for the Highlands. This brings us to the matter of how we react, when we come upon unfamiliar terrain that does not match the images we have learned to expect. While the winding towers of the bygone coal age are being preserved in the Ruhr, they may not be set up just anywhere. Here, the ideological potential of the word landscape comes to light, such as Hitler and his planner Alwin Seifert saw in German autobahn design, for example.

Initially, the term landscape belonged to the everyday jargon of politics; it denoted the land around a ruler or a city. Since such land came also to be painted, the term was adopted by landscape painters. Experts began to use the word also in an abstract sense, as in: the beautiful landscape, detached from the political landscape. This fostered integration of the legacy of the ancient classics: the topos of the *locus amoenus,* the charming place, at the origin of the "Hirtenlied" (Shepherd's Song)—precisely that genre of poetry devised by the first urban peoples after they had enslaved the last of the peasants: Happy people…!

After landscape had become a part of professional painters' jargon, travelers and tourists adopted it too: wherever they went, they discovered "landscapes," which basically meant that they found, on their travels, places looking very like those they had previously seen in pictures, or had conjured in their imagination. Writers described or constructed landscapes that increasingly bore traits of the "universally beautiful," such that readers could easily combine them with the "unpainted landscapes" of their own conjecture. An extreme example can be found at the start of *Wilhelm Meister's Journeymen Years,* where Goethe even provides the reader with staffage—the Holy Family on the run.

Laypeople mentally armed with the "images" of writers, especially of travel writers, begin to recognize what is "typical" of a landscape. "Landscape" takes on a new, everyday meaning, closer again to the old, political one: landscapes are the places where we spend our vacations. Hitherto the timeless *locus amoenus,* landscape now becomes an object of fashion and aesthetic depreciation. The history of tourism in the Alps can be seen as the discovery and the devastation of the landscape: around 1800, the major lakes; from 1840, the smaller and more remote ones in the mountains; next, the waterfalls, and then the higher valleys of Davos and St. Moritz, followed by the Bernina, Aletsch, and Furka glaciers, until finally, by the end of the nineteenth century, there was only one sensation left—the skiing season.

The most interesting means of gaining an idea of the typical landscape is the walk; or also, in this age of the car, the joyride. Interesting is the fact that the series of places approached on foot, or driven through, leaves an impression of a landscape that is never, as such, seen. The tourist visits Vézelay and the ruins of Cluny, takes a look at Beaune, tastes the wine and, once home, knows what the Burgundy region is like, what is typical there, and how the local people have ruined their landscape by evidently failing even to notice what is typical. The trip, the walk, and the information gained therefrom are of major significance for the "unpainted landscapes" in our mind's eye. So, now we can return to our primary topic, the minimal intervention.

Once we have accepted that the landscape is not an existent entity, but merely a mental construct colored by our cultural context, then this is bound to have an impact on our judgment of that art form which creates artificial environments for us: gardening.

The art of gardening, today, is not in a good state—or, to be more precise, for caution's sake: at least not on the continent of Europe in its official manifestation, the garden show. There, we can observe that maximal means are used: the bulldozer, special plant cultures, the extreme use of fertilizers, and the thoroughly arbitrary dispersion of earth. Topography, soil type, and irrigation no longer play a role; everything is possible, everywhere: springs and swamp vegetation on hilltops, steppe grasses in formerly wet valleys. As a result, everything can be combined: we find azaleas among steppe plants, giant tulips among dwarf conifers, ponds on slopes, and waterfalls in valley beds. In consequence, since everything is possible and combinable, the means used are so contradictory as to cancel one another out: the end result is a lack of effect. Since the effects remain ineffectual, the means are intensified—in the belief that the desired message will then be instantly clear to the viewer.

Twice, in recent history, garden art has found itself in this kind of hopeless situation. Each time, it was mavericks who lent it new, crucial momentum. The first time was when English poets and dilettantes replaced the formal garden with the landscape garden; the second time was when the architects of Art Nouveau and Modernism replaced the meanwhile routine landscape garden with the architectural garden. Implicit in the theory of minimal intervention is the premise that it is artists who liberate garden art from its entanglement with the maximal intervention.

The landscape gardens of the eighteenth century were hugely ambitious ventures, but they were executed according to the premise of minimal intervention. Lancelot "Capability" Brown acquired his nickname because he looked for locations that had the potential for all he envisioned yet whose original topography and vegetation could nonetheless be maintained.

The transformation of the Bergpark Wilhelmshöhe in Kassel, from a baroque garden to a landscape garden, involved a massive displacement of earth, but it still followed the method of minimal intervention. The Elector wished to renew the garden, but without destroying the work of his grandfather—a cascade of waterfalls, crowned by the giant statue of Hercules. The intervention consisted in inserting a "Gothic" castle into the upper left-hand area and the "ruin" of a Roman aqueduct lower down, on the right-hand side of the central axis: thus, the renowned S-shape was created and the untouched statue of Hercules became one among many features in the park's design. The same transformation is echoed in miniature in the formal center of the garden. Six paths describe a star shape around a grotto, without marring it. As for the visitor's idea of untouched nature, it is barely ruffled by the new design, thanks to the asymmetrical, snaking watercourse.

All the great parks of the eighteenth century attest the same fundamental paradox: landscape is represented by landscape. Symbols of landscape cannot be seen independently of the immediate impressions left by their original natural setting. Indeed, research has shown that many visitors to the English Garden in Munich, designed by Friedrich Ludwig von Sckell, believe that they are in an "original" (as in pristine) location, despite being at the heart of the city. Not that such direct representation of landscape by landscape expresses the minimal intervention, for the latter aims to influence the viewer's imagination by means of signs; when used consciously, in this context, the minimal intervention is a ploy of the artistic kind.

Bernard Lassus identified ordinary residents as landscape designers who use minimal intervention to bring an impression of infinite space to their small gardens. The fleeting gaze of a person with a middle-class background often reads garden gnomes, miniature houses, castles, and deer only in a literal sense. However, the most imaginative of suburban garden architects take such objects not at face value, but as potent symbols of distance and interrelationship: windmills and a ship are signs of wide, open spaces; miniature buildings and the plants around them represent the transition from man-made nature to untamed space.

In his own work, Lassus endeavors to follow the example set by the suburban landscape designers, using their private symbols as signifiers that can be grasped by the general public: for solely a common code can lend meaning to the design of a public park or garden. The greatest triumph, for Lassus, is when his intervention— the artifice—is taken to be real.

At the Federal Garden Show in Stuttgart, I saw landscape architects install a "natural" spring on a man-made hill, the roof of an autobahn tunnel; this turned the logical connection between underground watercourses and a spring completely on its head; the entire construct epitomized a maximal intervention. Lassus, who at a cursory glance may appear to do similar things, succeeds in breathing life into such artifice. One of his projects entailed designing a bridge over a highway that bisects a public park. He made the bridge resemble a cliff face, in part, and set a rustic-looking fountain on it. While, in Stuttgart, the attempt to "paper over the cracks" in a complex undertaking resulted in a gigantic intervention, Lassus's tongue-in-cheek citation of a rural fountain became a popular backdrop for wedding photos: it may be fake, but people accept the truth of it, on account of its poetic character.

Ian Hamilton Finlay's gardens are likewise characterized by minimal intervention: they are expressed by artistic symbols and use poetic inscriptions to communicate. With the latter medium, Ian Hamilton Finlay directly cites a cultural idiom. His inscription in stone of the words "See POUSSIN Hear LORRAIN" turns a tiny pond at a farm into a setting from classical painting. A stone lying in the grass and inscribed with Albrecht Dürer's initials evokes associations with the large lawn of the Albertina in Vienna. Ian Hamilton Finlay mediates between things normally considered opposites: the garden and the forest, the pond and the sea, the tranquility of the "charming place" and the battlefields of World War II; the virtues of farmers and the virtues of the French Revolution. Finally, the garden of Ian Hamilton Finlay sheds light on the relationship between nature and those who behold it. His inscriptions on tree trunks are allusions to Arcadian poetry and the custom of carving our names into the bark of a tree; to signage in a botanical garden and the labelling of nature—ventures that look to the future in this era of cultural shifts.

Science as a futile attempt to get close to nature is a recurring theme in Paul-Armand Gette's minimal interventions. His project for the Botanical Garden in Basel ranges from the expansion of clouds to small enamel labels on all the plants on an adjacent hill with the single inscription *"Plantago lanceolata, L."*: ribwort plantain, while with "Kassel—A Botanical Garden," he turned the entire city into a botanical garden by labelling even the plants sprouting from the cracks in the sidewalks with their Latin names. His latest minimal intervention, likewise on the theme of landscape, takes all the recently built art museums in Europe in its sights. Gette plans to install plastic water lilies in the hand wash basins of the public toilets of these exhibition venues, and to ironically inquire into where exactly landscape begins by hanging the sign "0 m" (Point Zero) on the toilet doors. Unfortunately, only the Centre Georges Pompidou in Paris has approved this complex installation with its allusions to a Monet landscape.

With an extremely minimal intervention in summer 1983, James Lee Byars interpreted the infinite expanse of landscape, naturally by means of a purely conceptual appeal to his audience. His performance under the title "A Drop of Black Perfume" was staged in the majestic surroundings of the Furka Pass, amid alpine meadows, cliffs, and vestiges of snow. The drop of a synthetic perfume landed on one of the millions of fragments of scree on the meadow, which the artist, dressed in a golden suit and hat, had selected with great care;

a brief performance, and one seemingly consisting in a fully absurd act. A drop of perfume is negligible compared to the scent of herbs and flowers wafting on the alpine air. Yet this mere split second of intervention transformed the entire Furka panorama.

Joseph Beuys' legacy in Kassel, the project "7000 Oak Trees," is a very ambitious and substantial work of art. I see it nonetheless as a minimal intervention, because it uses artistic means to communicate environmental problems. The constraints of politics and public order can be overcome by a maverick, an artist—by recourse not to violence, revolution, or subversive underground activity, but to ordinary, public, democratic procedures. In 1982, the international art show documenta 7 invited Beuys to erect a sculpture on Friedrichsplatz, directly in front of the main exhibition venue, the Museum Fridericianum. His sculpture consisted of a neat pile of seven thousand basalt blocks. In addition, Beuys explained that he wished to plant seven thousand trees on public land in Kassel, and that he would remove one basalt block from the sculpture and embed it alongside a tree, each time one was planted. The sculpture was thus programmed from the start to slowly vanish, and, simultaneously, to heighten public awareness of a new tree being planted in some city district for every block of stone that was carted off. The sculpture would be complete when it completely disappeared. The City of Kassel was now—as Beuys highlighted by punning on two similar German words—well forested *(gut verwaldet)*, hence, well governed *(gut verwaltet)*.

The political agenda driving Beuys's work rests on the assumption that any well-governed city should have a garden and parks department with a policy of planting trees wherever possible. The artist's proposal to plant seven thousand additional trees seemed completely absurd to the City of Kassel; it wasn't happy with the idea, but couldn't refuse a donation of this sort. The sculpture was already in place and its premature removal might alert the public to the fact that Beuys' seven thousand trees could go to another city. So, the administration had no choice but to accept this bequest, and it even supervised the plantings itself, to avoid further scandal. It had to launch a study of seven thousand sites for new plantings, after officially proclaiming that no such sites existed.

I'll return now, briefly, to the garden. It is certainly short-sighted, to say that we can learn from art directly. But we can learn from the principle of mediated expression, from minimal intervention. Recent gardening styles have revisited old paradoxes. The classicist tendency is fallible inasmuch as it is synchronous with classicist architecture, and the result is a rigid conformity between the styles of house and garden. The alternative, the ecological garden, throws up the same problems as the old landscape-style garden.

Nature is invisible and cannot be represented directly, but only through images. With our 500–1,000 square meter gardens, we cannot hope to save a rare plant species from extinction, but we can symbolize the beauty of untouched nature.

## From the Slide Archive of Annemarie and Lucius Burckhardt

p. 147

"Un air rosé" (Pink-tinted Air) was the name Bernard Lassus gave to his experiment with a tulip: he held within a bloom a strip of white paper, to demonstrate that the air glows pink even when nothing is physically altered: a fundamental premise of the minimal intervention.

pp. 148–49

Joseph Beuys, "7000 Oak Trees," Kassel, 1982–87: a substantial work of art yet still a minimal intervention, for Beuys used artistic means to communicate environmental problems. The constraints of politics and public order can be overcome by a maverick, an artist—by recourse not to violence, revolution, or subversive underground activity, but to ordinary, public, democratic procedures.

pp. 150–51

Ian Hamilton Finlay "Osiers/Osiris," tree panels, at Stonypath, Little Sparta, since 1966; and a stone inscribed "F. Hadler," Furka, 1987: Finlay's inscriptions in tree trunks allude both to Arcadian poetry and our custom of carving names into tree bark. Such interpretations in stone or wood reframe our views of the landscape, provoking a shift in consciousness and a new way of seeing the environment.

pp. 152–53

With "Kassel—A Botanical Garden" at the documenta urbana—making visible in 1982, Paul-Armand Gette labeled even the weeds sprouting from cracks in the sidewalks with their Latin names, thus turning the streets and open spaces of the city into a single botanical garden. Another installation, in Furka in 1992, was 0 m (Point Zero): Where does the landscape begin? Everything we see before us can be named scientifically; if we look up, at some point a landscape comes into view.

p. 154

In "A Drop of Black Perfume" (1983), James Lee Byars staged an extremely minimal intervention to interpret an infinite landscape, naturally only in the mind's eye of his spectators. Amid alpine meadows, rocks, and vestiges of snow in the grandiose Furka Pass, he placed a drop of perfume on a granite block. Here, Annemarie Burckhardt's photograph shows Byars dressed in a suit of gold and a black hood for his second performance on the Furka, "The Introduction of the Sages to the Alps" (1984).

## Four Walks with Annemarie and Lucius Burckhardt

p. 156
"0 m (Point Zero) Walk," Kassel-Wilhelmshöhe, 1985. Ten metal frames installed in the park enabled walkers to view and critique various views of the landscape, as they would a painting. The label seen here on the right-hand margin states: "This image depicts the Cestius Pyramid. It is intended to remind us of Ancient Rome. There, the wealthy Cestius had a pyramid built for himself, to remind him of Ancient Egypt."

p. 157
"The Voyage to Tahiti" of 1987 led to a disused military training ground near Kassel. At various points on the walk, an actor read aloud texts by Georg Forster, who visited Tahiti with Captain Cook in 1772. It was a Tahitian soundtrack for views of the Dönche in Kassel, a spot for which Forster's descriptions of the paradise isle seemed equally apt.

p. 158
"The Villa Medici Travel Agency," Rome, 1997. "Goethe, Winckelmann, & Co., when they took a walk here, saw a very different picture than we do." (Lucius Burckhardt, at the first official opening of the Villa Medici Gardens to the general public.) Together with a group of Roman artists he devised a series of ten walks to explore the sides of Rome never seen on picture postcards.

p. 159
"The Zebra Crossing," Kassel, 1993. The Roving Gaze. Strollology, the science of walking, seeks out locations and other living things and experiments with rediscovering what it sees. To see is to adopt new perspectives, to try out new ways of looking, to be open to the unfamiliar, to identify which elements disrupt, and to make mistakes and remark to ourselves that we do. Strollology aims to foster a different understanding of time and space.

# Biographies

**Lucius Burckhardt,** *1925 in Davos, Dr. phil. in Basel, was from 1955 a research assistant at the Social Research Center of the University of Munster in Dortmund. Following a guest lectureship in 1959 at the Ulm School of Design in Germany, held several teaching positions from 1961 to 1973, also as guest lecturer in sociology in the architecture department at the Swiss Federal Institute of Technology (ETH Zurich). In parallel, was editor of the Swiss architectural journal *Werk* (1962–72), and chairman of the *Deutscher Werkbund* (1976–83). Was appointed professor of the socio-economy of urban systems at Kassel University of Applied Sciences in 1973; was a member both of the German Academy for Urban and Regional Planning, and (1987–89) the founding advisory board of the HbK Saar University of Art and Design, and also founding dean of the design faculty at Bauhaus University Weimar (1992–94). His outstanding achievements in the fields of science, sociology, and aesthetics were honored with the Chevalier dans l'Ordre des Arts et des Lettres, the Hessian Culture Prize (1994), the Federal Prize for Designers (1995), and the Design Prize Switzerland (2001). Lucius Burckhardt died in 2003, in his hometown Basel.

**Markus Ritter,** *1954 in Basel, is a biologist. Founded the political party Grüne Alternative Basel (Green Alternative Basel) together with Lucius and Annemarie Burckhardt, in 1986. Was a member of Basel-Stadt Canton parliament (1988–2001), in the final years also its president, and later a member of its policy unit (2006–18). Meanwhile retired. Numerous projects, seminars, and articles with Lucius Burckhardt on landscape, nature, and environmental issues, from 1987 on; also publishes in books and professional journals on environmental and conservation history, ornithology, and botany. Has been involved since 2012 in archiving and publishing the work of Lucius and Annemarie Burckhardt.

**Martin Schmitz,** *1956 in Hamm/Westphalia. Studied architecture, urban planning, and landscape planning under Lucius Burckhardt at the University of Kassel. Wrote *Über die Kultur der Imbißbude* (1983), about snack bar culture. Curated the film program at documenta 8, Kassel (1987); the Dilettantism Conference, Görlitz (1995); the exhibition *Die Tödliche Doris—Kunst*, Berlin (1999); the international congress "Spaziergangswissenschaft: Sehen, erkennen und planen" (Strollology; see, recognize, plan), Frankfurt (2008); and the Lucius Burckhardt Conventions, Kassel (2014/2017). Launched the publishing house Martin Schmitz Verlag in 1989, with a list covering architecture, urban planning, art, film, design, music, and literature. Was appointed professor at the Kunsthochschule Kassel in 2013.

# Sources

*Der kleinstmögliche Eingriff oder Die Rückführung der Planung auf das Planbare* (**The Minimal Intervention** or Returning Planning to the Planable, unpublished manuscript, 1979–81).

**Der kleinste Eingriff** — L'intervention minimale — **The Minimal Intervention**, a seminar held in post-earthquake Belice (Sicily), Sept. 10–12, 1981. In: *Bauwelt* 73/4, 1982, pp. 127–30. — In: Fachbereich Architektur der Gesamthochschule Kassel (ed.), *Architektur für den Nutzer—Gebrauchsarchitektur (The Teaching of Architecture with People in Mind)*. 6th Report on outcomes of the EAAE workshop of November 1982, Kassel, 1984, pp. 60–64. — In: Bazon Brock (ed.) *Die Kinder fressen ihre Revolution*, Du Mont: Cologne 1985, pp. 241–47. — In: Silvan Blumenthal, Martin Schmitz (eds.) *Design ist unsichtbar. Entwurf, Gesellschaft und Padagogik*, Martin Schmitz Verlag: Berlin 2012, pp. 297–304; *Design is Invisible. Planning, Education, and Society*, Birkhäuser: Basel 2017, pp. 273–79.

**Minimal Intervention** In: Simon Cutts (ed.), *The Unpainted Landscape*, Coracle Press: London 1987, pp. 96–109.

# Books by Lucius Burckhardt

Jesko Fezer, Martin Schmitz (eds.), *Who Plans the Planning? Architecture, Politics, and Mankind*, Birkhäuser: Basel 2020.

Silvan Blumenthal, Martin Schmitz (eds.), *Design is Invisible. Planning, Education, and Society*, Birkhäuser: Basel 2017.

Markus Ritter, Martin Schmitz (eds.), *Why Is Landscape Beautiful? The Science of Strollology*, Birkhäuser: Basel 2015.

Jesko Fezer, Martin Schmitz (eds.), Lucius Burckhardt Writings. *Rethinking Man-made Environments. Politics, Landscape & Design*, Springer: Vienna 2012.

www.lucius-burckhardt.org

For translations into Italian, see Quodlibet; into French, see Flammarion.

# Index

# Photo Credits

All images are from the slide archive of Annemarie & Lucius Burckhardt, which is now held by the University Library Basel.